MAY 2005

ISBN 0-615-12364-3

Published 2003 by The Delius Society - Philadelphia Branch, Inc.
with the support of The Delius Trust, London

The Delius Society - Philadelphia Branch, Inc.
3432, Bleigh Avenue,
Philadelphia, PA 19136

Acknowledgements

I wish to acknowledge with thanks the following publishers for their kind permission to reprint excerpts from their publications: Faber & Faber Ltd., and Dover Publications, Inc., for the quotations commencing *Now let's clear the air* and *I want you to imagine* from pages 25 and 132 of *Delius as I knew him* by Eric Fenby, revised edition published by Faber & Faber Ltd., London 1981; W. W. Norton & Company Inc., and Schomburg Center for Research in Black Culture for the quotations commencing *In slavery, some holler* and *When we wanted* from pages 117 & 121 of Eileen Southern's *Readings in Black Music*, W. W. Norton & Company Inc., New York, 1971; Simon & Schuster for the quotation beginning *But he do for hisself mostly*, from page 267 of the *The Other Florida*. Reprinted with permission of Scribner, a imprint of Simon & Schuster Adult Publishing Group from *The Other Florida* by Gloria Jahoda. Copyright © 1967 by Gloria Jahoda; also to Simon & Schuster for the quotation commencing *Philip (Heseltine) had rekindled* from page 180 of Gloria Jahoda's *The Road to Samarkand*, reprinted with permission of Scribner, an imprint of Simon & Schuster Adult Publishing Group from *The Road to Samarkand* by Gloria Jahoda. Copyright © 1969 by Gloria Jahoda.

The New York Philharmonic Orchestra for permission to quote W. H. Humiston's program notes for their concert on November 26th., 1915 commencing *When he was about twenty* and *The theme of the slow movement.* Shirley, Lady Beecham and the Sir Thomas Beecham Trust Ltd., for the quotation commencing *After lunch one day Frederick,* from *Frederick Delius* by Sir Thomas Beecham, published by Hutchinson & Company (London) and Knopf (New York); and Professor Bruce Jackson for permission to quote the opening measures of the song *Make a Longtime Man feel bad* from his *Wake Up Dead Man: Afro-American Worksongs from Texas Prisons* published by Harvard University Press.

I would also like to thank the following music publishers for their kind permission to quote numerous examples in this study from the works of Frederick Delius.

Stainer & Bell (London) for their kind permission to quote from

North Country Sketches	*Concerto for Violin and Violoncello*
Dance Rhapsody No 2	*Violin Concerto*
String Quartet	*Summer Evening*

Boosey & Hawkes Ltd., for their kind permission to quote from the following works in their catalogue:

FLORIDA SUITE
© Copyright 1963 by Hawkes & Son (London) Ltd.
Copyright Renewed
Reprinted by permission of Boosey & Hawkes, Inc.

IRMELIN
© Copyright 1953, 1955 by The Delius Trust.
Copyright Renewed.
Reprinted by permission of Boosey & Hawkes, Inc.Sole Agent

KOANGA
© Copyright 1935, 1974, 1980 by The Delius Trust.
Copyright Renewed
Reprinted by permission of Boosey & Hawkes, Inc.. Sole Agent.

ROMANCE FOR CELLO AND PIANO
© Copyright 1975 by Boosey & Hawkes Music Publishers Ltd.
Reprinted by permission of Boosey & Hawkes, Inc.

PIANO CONCERTO
© Copyright 1951 by Hawkes & Son (London) Ltd.
Copyright renewed
Reprinted by permission of Boosey & Hawkes, Inc.

APPALACHIA
© Copyright Revised Ed. 1951 by Hawkes & Son (London) Ltd. Copyright Renewed.
Reprinted by permission of Boosey & Hawkes, Inc.

Universal Edition, Vienna for their kind permission to quote from the following works:

Delius SONGS OF SUNSET
Used with kind permission of European American Music
Distributors LLC, sole U.S. & Canadian agent for
Universal Edition A.G., Vienna.

Delius BRIGG FAIR
Used with kind permission of European American Music
Distributors LLC, sole U.S. & Canadian agent for
Universal Edition A.G., Vienna.

Delius IN A SUMMER GARDEN
Used with kind permission of European American Music
Distributors LLC, sole U.S. & Canadian agent for
Universal Edition A.G., Vienna.

Delius A DANCE RHAPSODY
Used with kind permission of European American Music
Distributors LLC, sole U.S. & Canadian agent for
Universal Edition A.G., Vienna.

Delius THE SONG OF THE HIGH HILLS
Used with kind permission of European American Music
Distributors LLC, sole U.S. & Canadian agent for
Universal Edition A.G., Vienna.

Every attempt has been made to clear copyright. Any oversight will be corrected.

On a more personal level, I should like to express gratitude to Jennifer and Bruce Rogers of Richmond Hill, Ontario for their help in proof reading; Robert Threlfall, *Delian extraordinary*, of the Delius Trust London for his encouragement and support particularly at the outset and the completion of this eighteen year journey; Bill Marsh of the Delius Society, Philadelphia, whose work as editor and whose interest in the revision and extension of the original paper was definitely paramount for the completion of the study; the library of the University of Oregon at Eugene for their help in acquiring materials in the opening stages of the research; the various public libraries of New York, particularly the Brooklyn Public Library who for twelve years have supplied most of material necessary for the revision of the original paper, but also to the Queens Public Library, the New York Public Library and of course the Schomburg Center for Research in Black Culture. Lastly, I wish to thank my wife Olive without whose support and help nothing would have been accomplished.

Contents

vi

PART FIVE / *Discussion of individual works.*

EPILOGUE

Preface

This study is a revision and enlargement of a paper entitled *The Influence of Black American Music on the Works of Frederick Delius: fact or nostalgia?* given originally at the 27th College Music Society Annual Meeting, Nashville, Tennessee, on October 5th, 1984. Taking advantage of my residence in New York, with its very fine public library system and the nation-wide inter-library loan, I decided in 1996 to totally revise the original.

My decision to work on the project was caused by hearing a respected Delius authority state that he thought there was little or no Afro-American influence whatever in FD's music, despite the composer's various comments to the contrary; his reasoning was that FD was being either nostalgic or else wished to surprise people.[1] This statement intrigued me. My original approach to the project was on the purely subjective level; namely I searched for any section of FD's music that sounded Afro-American, and in many cases it turned out to be the best way to go. Often however it was not exactly clear why the section in question sounded as though it was inspired by his years spent in the USA. When studying the works of an intuitive composer such as FD, it is tempting to make subjective pronouncements, but I feel that his stature as a composer is diminished by not using objective reasoning whenever possible.

It soon became apparent that I would find few complete Afro-American melodies in his works, since on the whole FD, like most composers of his generation, preferred open-ended forms. Also for example, even the *Appalachia* variation theme is nowhere to be found in any collection of songs published in the USA. It became apparent that he preferred secular songs and instrumental dances to spirituals; this also presented a problem since whereas about a thousand spirituals from the nineteenth century or earlier have survived, it wasn't until 1923 that the first extended work devoted to secular song was printed, namely Dorothy Scarborough's *On the trail of Negro Folk Songs*. By all accounts, the secular tradition was very strong in the eighteen hundreds, but being a form of popular music, thousands of pieces would have been created, had their place in the sun, and then except for a small handful, disappeared forever without a trace. I was therefore obliged to enter the world of micro-structures and to spend much time checking through the collections of Afro-American vocal music in order to discover the rhythmic units, note patterns, preferred pitches and scales that made the world of nineteenth century Black American music so unique. Then I ascertained if FD had any preferences for these devices; the results from the start were very encouraging. In many cases I felt as though my methods mimicked those of a detective, and in some cases I regretted intruding on a private part of the composer's life. But nonetheless I believe my conclusions are as objective as I can possibly to make them.

This study is divided into five main sections:

i)   FD's recorded contact with Afro-Americans and their music.

ii)   Characteristics of European, African and Afro-American music.

iii)   Harmonic, melodic and rhythmic devices common to both FD's works and those of Afro-Americans.

iv)   Different categories of Delian motives and melodies.

v)   Discussion of individual works.

I have used 'point' form throughout in the manner of an encyclopedia in order to make for easy reference. There are a large number of musical examples given in the appendix, thereby saving the reader time spent searching through the scores or collections of spirituals. I have tried to consider every possible similarity between the two types of music discussed, even though in some cases it might appear too obvious to mention. I have also tried to keep personal opinions to a minimum.

The works of FD selected for use in this study consist mostly of those currently in print and therefore easily available to the reader. There are a number of orchestral works which I chose to omit since at first hearing they seemed to contain few if any Afro-American characteristics; these include *Paris, Life's Dance, Eventyr, Cynara,* and *Over the hills and far away.* On the other hand, the two extended works *The Magic Fountain* and *Fennimore and Gerda* appear to contain a great deal of influence from the composer's period in Florida and Virginia, but due to the constraints of time and for personal reasons I decided not to include them, but to produce an extended paper devoted to them at a later date.

My love of FD's music was born at the age of sixteen when first I heard the English Rhapsody *Brigg Fair,* and my respect for his inspiration and technique as a composer has continued to grow over the years. I therefore hope that this text will be of interest to those who have a similar affection for his music as well as those interested in discovering more of nineteenth century Afro-American music.

DEREK E. HEALEY

Brooklyn, New York
May 2001

Some five months after completing this work, Robert Threlfall of the Delius Trust, published in *The Delius Society Journal, Autumn 2001, Number 130,* an important article entitled *An Early Manuscript Reappears* which discussed a previously unknown manuscript of FD containing sketches of Negro folk song arrangements estimated by Mr. Threlfall as being written in the years 1889-90. This discovery, I feel, has validated the methods used throughout the present study. Not wishing to rework parts of my text, I have inserted parenthetical notes regarding the discovery in two places: in Section 64 *Group VI: Irmelin/Koanga/Appalachia Theme,* and Section 74 *Koanga* [1895/7]: the original assertions have remained unaltered.

DEREK E. HEALEY

Brooklyn, New York
November 2001

PART ONE / *FD's contact with Afro-Americans and their music.*

1 Early Years

Delius's first contact with American Music was in performances of blackfaced Minstrel Shows which were very popular in England during his childhood. This contact with mainly white-composed imitative Afro-American music obviously left an impression, since Sir Francis Watson recalled that as a young boy, Delius mounted a Christie Minstrel Show of his own and even mentions one of the songs sung, *Shine, shine Moon*.2 There is a slight possibility that he came in contact with Afro-Caribbean children during his period of study at the very progressive International School at Isleworth, London during the years 1878/80.3

2 FD in Florida

In 1881 FD entered his father's woollen business and, with a gradually diminishing amount of success, was pushed to the verge of a nervous breakdown. Resulting from this he managed to persuade his father to lease him an orange farm at Solano Grove, and on March 2nd, 1884 he sailed for Florida via New York with another young rebel Charles Douglas. The music he would have heard on the journey would have included stevedore songs at Jacksonville and Fernandina as well as male quartet popular songs, shanties, soundings, and riverboat songs on the St. Johns River since it was policy on the DeBarry steamers to encourage black deck-hands to sing as much as possible for the pleasure of the passengers.4 The passing of these floating concert halls were to be a source of great enjoyment for the young errant Orange Farmer.

Another frequent source of musical enjoyment for Delius was the regular evening concerts given by his foreman Elbert Anderson together with his wife and sister-in-law, and possibly a few other plantation workers.5 We are fortunate enough to have an account of these events given to Gloria Jahoda by Elbert Anderson's sister-in-law, Julia Sanks in 1966.6 Jahoda begins by asking the 90-year-old Julia Sanks about the housekeeping:

> *'But he do for hisself mostly, like I say, I redd up the house. Maybe he don't care what he eat if he can be at his piano or his fiddle. Long as he make his music, he just don't mind what else. He didn't have no conveniences. He didn't care about the fruits, neither. He didn't do yard work to speak of. It was a trouble to Elbert, and a worry. He weren't much for hard work, Mister Delius, and that's a fact. Just that music. I ain't heard nothing like it and that's a fact. I dis remember what I sang to him except the hymns. You know - 'No Trouble in that Land where I'm Bound' and 'Jesus is Comin' Again'. It was Elbert mostly he wanted to hear.'*

Incidentally I've managed to trace four totally different versions of *Jesus is Comin' Again* - all from white gospel hymn books; none of these seem to contain anything of interest to a composer. I have had no luck with *No Trouble in that Land where I'm Bound*.

This totally foreign music together with the luxuriant vegetation and scents produced in Delius such an impact that there and then he decided to become a composer and to introduce these new sounds to the world of classical music. His interest in orange farming waned, and after a three month period of seeing not a single white person, he started to have composition and counterpoint lessons from a prematurely retired New York organist, Thomas Ward. At the end of July an emissary from his father, a Mr Tatterfield, arrived to report on the state of affairs. His report stated that Fritz divided his time between 'Furious Energy' at music and sitting in a boat on the river listening to Elbert Anderson playing his banjo and singing slave songs.7 At this time Delius would also have heard field-hollers from his plantation workers, as well as the music from passing sternwheelers.

1

Early in 1885 he moved to Jacksonville, where, according to Gloria Jahoda, Fritz made some visits to the black suburb of La Villa listening to church services and probably hearing the famed Cornet Band, as well as more Male Quartets sometimes called Street Corner Quartets.8

3 Leaves Florida for Virginia, New York and Leipzig

After spending 18 months at Solano Grove and Jacksonville, Delius departed for Danville, Virginia, with the hope of making enough money teaching to travel to Leipzig in order to study composition. He stayed at Danville for eight months and continued his study of Black music. This time it was the work songs and spirituals he heard in the tobacco stemmery buildings where apparently as many as three hundred workers sang at any one time. Almost certainly they would have used the early antebellum style of ensemble singing discussed later; he also heard spirituals sung by the cook of his friend Robert Phifer.9 After spending a short time in New York, in June, 1886, he left for Leipzig via Liverpool. Upon receiving his diploma from the Leipzig Conservatory he settled in Paris where he made artistic contact with such important figures as Grieg, Gaugin, Munch and Strindberg.

In 1897 he decided to return to the U.S. in order to dispose of Solano Grove, give a few concerts and renew an acquaintance with an American publisher; and also, Grainger mentions in *The Personality of Frederick Delius,* to renew contact with an Afro-American sweetheart; [10 he later added that a child had been born of the union - a fact corroborated by Eric Fenby.11   FD was unsuccessful in finding both the girl and the child. This venture lasted until May, during which time he visited Danville, but spent most of his time working on the early version of the *Piano Concerto* at Solano Grove; his disposition had changed somewhat from his early days according to both Anderson and Sanks.12 He returned to Paris for another two years before settling down at Grez-sur-Loing with the artist Jelka Rosen; they were married on September 23rd, 1903, and except for one year spent in England during the First World War and a few summers in Norway, he spent the rest of his days in this small picturesque village some 40 miles south of Paris.

4 Florida in retrospect

Delius frequently spoke of the effect his American sojourn had upon his compositions;[13 for example Eric Fenby reports that after listening to a particularly fine radio performance of *Brigg Fair* by Beecham, Delius said: *Now let's clear the air and play that record of the Revellers 'Ol Man River'.*14 Fenby continues:

This and other such records gave him great pleasure, for the singing was reminiscent of the way his negroes used to sing out in Florida, when as a young orange-planter he had often sat up far into the night, smoking cigar after cigar, and listening to their subtle improvisations in harmony. "They showed a truly wonderful sense of musicianship and harmonic resource in the instinctive way in which they treated a melody," he added, " and, hearing their singing in such romantic surroundings, it was then and there that I first felt the urge to express myself in music."

We have similar comments made to Beecham, [15 Warlock [16 and Elgar, [17 but perhaps the most moving is that found in the final paragraph of the announcement of FD's death in a London daily newspaper of June 11th, 1934, which states *and (FD) said he owed a great debt to the negro music he heard when he was working at an orange-grove in Florida in the 'eighties.18* Beecham has a further interesting anecdote which etches permanently Delius's love of this music. The event occurred in 1896 when Delius was discussing his proposed new opera *Koanga* with C.F. Keary and Jelka.19

After lunch one day Frederick, to the delight of his two friends bought out a fiddle on which he played many Negro melodies, some of which he was minded to introduce into the work under way.

In other words, I think it safe to say that there was no doubt that Frederick Delius was exceedingly moved by the Afro-American music he had heard as a young man in the United States.

PART TWO / *Characteristics of European, African and Afro-American music.*

5 European influences

Before starting to discuss 19th-century Afro-American music, I think it important to stress that that the main fabric of FD's music was basically Post-Wagnerian with other techniques learned from Grieg and Richard Strauss. From an early age he was deeply affected by the music of Chopin and Wagner, particularly *Lohengrin* which he heard at Covent Garden in his teens.20 Later he developed a liking for Grieg; he gave a performance of a Grieg *Violin Sonata* at Filey in Yorkshire in 1879 when he was 17.21 To this list of lifelong influences, we can add the name of Bach, to whose music he was introduced by Thomas Ward in 1884. Eric Fenby, in his record jacket notes to *Life's Dance*, makes the statement that Delius had carefully studied the works of Strauss; he had four of his scores in his library: *Don Juan, Till Eulenspiegel, Ein Heldenleben* and *Zarathustra.* Incidentally being a composer who was totally self-supporting he could afford the luxury of disliking the music of numerous hallowed figures including Haydn, Mozart, Beethoven, Brahms, Schoenberg and Hindemith.22 Eric Fenby remarks that from Grieg FD developed his turn of modulation, from Chopin his shape of melodic lines and from Wagner his sense of flow; [23 to this formidable trio Grainger adds the influence of Bach, Debussy and the music of Afro-Americans. Obviously FD was largely still a part of the European tradition.24

However, bearing this in mind, his use of Afro-American color and techniques could be considerable. For example the American composer H. T. Burleigh writing of Dvorak's *New World Symphony* states:

There is a tendency in these days to ignore the Negro elements in the "New World Symphony", shown by the fact that many of those who were able in 1893 to find traces of Negro musical color all through the symphony, though the workmanship and treatment of the themes was and is Bohemian, now cannot find anything in the whole four movements that suggests any local or Negro influence, though there is no doubt at all that Dr. Dvorak was deeply impressed by the old Negro spirituals and also by the Foster Songs.25

The same is obviously true of many of Delius's works, much of the old plantation feel of *Appalachia* or *Koanga* is no longer evident to modern audiences. Percy Grainger for example took exception to the cadence of the main theme in the first *Dance Rhapsody* saying that the theme is typically Northern European with its jaunty rhythm and its use of the sharpened fourth but that the cadence is Afro-American. To me the whole theme is pure Delius, but to Grainger writing in 1934 there was 'ethnic confusion' here.26

Any Afro-Americanisms FD decided to add to his compositions would have to fit within this European compositional framework. He chose not to use many of the forms of Afro-American music, such as call-and-response patterns or elaborate rhythmical ornamentation over a moving rhythmic or harmonic background, as did Gershwin in the opera *Porgy and Bess* fifty years later. The characteristics he did use however were mainly melodic devices, characteristic rhythmic units found within these melodies and to a certain lesser extent harmonic characteristics.

6 The characteristics of Afro-American music
At this time I think it would not be amiss to list generally accepted Afro-American musical characteristics; these are a result of commonly held beliefs, my own observations and the writings of the following:

Henry Edward Krehbiel's *Afro-American Folksongs*
Portia Maultesby's *Afro-American Religious Music - 1619-1861*
George Robinson Ricks's *Some aspects of the Religious Music of the US Negro*
Bruno Nettl's *Folk and Traditional Music of the Western Continents*
and the writings of Mieczyslaw Kolinski and Alan Lomax.

Regarding the overall structure, antiphonal music (call-and-response) predominates. Polyphony is very common. Improvisation (variation) is also important particularly in the solo voice. Both a slightly husky and raspy singing tone are favored. Portamenti (blue-notes) are prevalent.

Rhythm (tempo giusto) is important and usually has an singularly undeviating tempo, since it has a very close relationship to dance. Syncopation (cakewalk, snaps and Latin rhythms) is also common. Triplets and dotted notes are favored as is duple time. There is an almost total absence of triple and compound time in music from the predominantly English-speaking areas of the USA. A rhythmic, frequently instrumental, accompaniment is normally present.

The most common scale structures were the anhemitonic pentatonic, hexatonic and heptatonic major scales, the natural minor scale as well as the Dorian and Mixolydian modes. Blue notes are also characteristic on the third, fifth, and seventh scale degrees: the sharpened fourth frequently gives a Lydian feel to a phrase. It was also common to change modes within a song using the 'shift' technique from Africa, to be discussed in section 42.

Three general melodic shapes predominate in early Afro-American melodies: the descending or tumbling melodic line, upper arch shape phrases, and a flat structure using a few closely related pitches. Repeated notes are common as is a rocking motion, oscillating between two near or adjacent pitches. Phrase lengths are shorter and more repetitive than those found in Western European folk music. Accompanying ostinato phrases are common only in music of the antebellum period.

7 The gradual disappearance of many African characteristics

All of the above mentioned techniques and preferences came over from Africa, but purely rhythmic instrumental techniques dropped out early on; e.g. complex rhythmic polyphony, polyrhythms, hemiola, hocket, use of drums in groups of three. Performances became far shorter; in Africa, composite musical forms frequently lasted up to twelve hours. The use of African purely instrumental background continuum: drums, bells or the m'bira, also disappeared early on with the total disappearance of the traditional instrumental ensemble, and as a result, melodic ostinatos became less important but continued to be used until the present time in Jubilee Hymns and Gospel Songs. A good example of this is the repeated sixteenth-note *'tell it'* in the bass part of *Father Abraham* found in *Calhoun Plantation Songs* of Emily Hallowell (1901). Any Asian influences obviously ceased, principally those from Indonesia, India and the Arab world.

Triple and compound time were very common in Africa, but apart from vocal and instrumental music from the American French-speaking areas, these had almost totally disappeared in the USA. When triple time did reappear as in Gospel songs such as Thomas A. Dorsey's laid-back *Take my hand, precious Lord* (1938) - the outside influence was now the white 19th-century Revivalist movement.

Pendulum melodies, organum, two-voiced rounds, and a solo singer improvising melodies over a fast repetitive melodic accompaniment also quickly disappeared. Complex melodic polyphony was replaced by simpler homophonic structures. Common African scales such as *do-re-sol-do* have disappeared altogether. The scale *do-mi-sol-la-do* lived on only in work songs, riverboat songs and 19th-century folk songs. The various forms of the anhemitonic pentatonic scale however remained in both religious and secular music right up to the 20th century. The older antebellum style of choral performance, with all performers improvising accompanying counter melodies, continued in pockets until the middle of the 20th century. Western style harmony began to dominate the melodic lines with melodies and improvisations frequently outlining chords, particularly in Jubilee and Gospel Hymns; this is particularly true of jazz.

Perhaps the element that has remained most stubbornly African is the practice of solo improvisation against a harmonic 20th-century choral or instrumental background, as in Gospel, Rhythm & Blues, and Jazz. From the rhythmic point of view, syncopation is still important, although the units have changed over time. Even taking all this into account, Afro-American music is just as unique today as it was in the 1880s; it doesn't take a second to decide on the ethnic origin of a singer or choir. The tone and performance practices may have changed somewhat but still remain Afro-American. It is of course possible that in time the style may partially revert to the African original as more and more black musicians study ensemble drumming such as can be heard, for example, in Street Fairs in the larger American cities.

8 River (rowing) songs

Probably the oldest solo or possibly small ensemble songs which FD would have heard with any degree of frequency are those which were used as an aid to rowing on America's rivers before the coming of steamships; their style has been well documented by two 19th-century commentators, W. H. Russell [27 and James Hungerford.28 Both writers commented on the sorrowful nature of these work songs; Hungerford noted their 'inexpressibly plaintive' character, while Russell commented on the 'quaint expression and melancholy' exhibited in them. When questioned on this, the oarsman in James Hungerford's *The Old Plantation* responded *De boat-songs is always dat way, marster*.29 The field of river songs was further explored by Dorothy Wheeler in her *Steamboatin' Days*. This enlightening volume contains songs mainly learnt in the final two or three decades of the 19th century, and so the texts were mainly devoted to songs from the age of the sternwheelers as well as songs from the earlier era such as *Woman, Woman, I seen yo' Man* [126]. Allen, Ware and Garrisons's *Slave Songs of the United States* contains what must be regarded as the archetypal rowing song, complete with snap-rhythms - *Lay this Body Down* [32].

FD's use of material from this genre was limited, since neither he or his music was of an overtly sorrowful or melancholy cast. Despite the fact that he must have heard these or similar songs frequently, he would have had little desire to include them in his work; nevertheless I believe he did adapt *Woman, Woman, I seen yo' Man* as the opening theme of the *Piano Concerto*.

9 Scales favored by Afro-Americans

I have included the result of a study made by Henry Edward Krehbiel in his 1914 *Afro-American Folksongs*, since the information contained would have changed little since the period of FD's residence in the US. Krehbiel's study concerns the scales employed in the 527 songs and spirituals available at the time. I have rearranged the order to make clearer their degree of use.

Ordinary Major	311	59%
Pentatonic	111	21%
Major without seventh*	78	14.8%
Ordinary Minor (Natural)	62	11.7%
Major without fourth*	45	8.5%
Minor without sixth*	34	6.4%
'Mixed and Vague'	23	4.3%
Major with flatted seventh (Mixolydian)	20	3.7%
Minor with raised seventh (Harmonic)	19	3.6%
Minor with raised sixth (Dorian)	8	1.5%

(* These hexatonic scales could be described as half-pentatonic since in each, one of the two semi-tones has been omitted - DH)

Books published since that date show little variance with the above listing and include four important collections which I feel should be mentioned; two of which have a 'time capsule' feel to them. The first being *Befo' de War Spirituals* collected by E. A. McIlhenny in 1933 from the singing of workers on his isolated sugar plantation on Avery Island, Louisiana; many had not been notated before, most of them having a Revivalist feel. Another is Lydia Parrish's *Slave Songs of the Georgia Sea Islands*, an important collection notated with accompanying ATB parts in 1942 and which contain many songs which have an 18th-century English feel to them with no blue notes notated. The other important texts include Dorothy Scarborough's *On the Trail of Negro Folk Songs* of 1925, an important collection of secular songs, and *American Negro Songs* (1940) by John W. Work which contains many songs previously collected but does include more secular songs than the texts used by Krehbiel.

10 Meter in African and Afro-American song and dance

The vast majority of 19th-century Afro-American songs from the English speaking areas of the US are in 2/4 or 4/4. Triple and compound duple songs and dances were quite common however in French speaking areas.30 There is no rarity of triple and compound times in Ghanaian music, since in J. H. Kwabena Nketia's text *The Music of Africa,* choral or vocal music appears to be mainly in 6/8; some 54% of the melodies quoted are in 6/8 and 22% in 3/4; these figures are not exact since a number of the songs make much use of hemiola thereby making the choice of time a matter of preference.

An interesting aside into the use of triple and duple times is given by A. M. Jones in his 1959 text *Studies of African Music* which deals primarily with the music of East Africa (Northern Rhodesia). He mentions the absence of a European lilt from triple time; although both 6/8 and 3/8 are frequently used in vocal and instrumental music, they are simply patterns of six or three beats and nothing more, He also tells a delightful story of an attempt to teach East African children a 6/8 Morris Dance; the children would invariably dance it in 2/4 against the accordion's compound time! A. M. Jones states that a fundamental characteristic of African music is the principle of three against two, this has almost totally disappeared from Afro-American music.

Perhaps the African use of triple and compound time is a relatively recent development which has developed since the diaspora and that the use of these times in French dominated areas is the result of French folk influence. Alternatively, at one time it may have been normal in East Africa to both dance and sing in duple time when instruments played in triple and/or compound time. Whatever the reason, Afro-American vocal music is primarily in simple duple or quadruple time with the proviso that the use of compound time is always present in order to give a 'swing' characteristic, as are the use of triplets.

11 Afro-American Ornamentation

Since early texts notated only the basic melody and made no attempt to notate the decoration of each verse, a short study of this very complex art has been included based on my own observations and songs found in two late 20th-century texts, Bruce Jackson's *Wake Up Dead Man* (worksongs from a Texas Prison) and Jeff Todd Titon's *Early Downhome Blues* (notations of early 20th-century Blues recordings), as well as field hollers mostly notated in the 1930s. The degree of ornamentation varies immensely from song to song, but certain patterns crop up constantly including the following;

i)   Both long [half or quarter note] and short [sixteenth note] stepwise appoggiaturas.

ii)   Descending and ascending appoggiaturas, jumping a third at a song's cadence.

iii) Oscillation between notes a second or a third apart, and in some instances, between a blue note and the note of resolution.

iv)   Repeated notes, mainly eighth and quarter notes.

v)   Snap rhythms, normally a sixteenth note followed by a dotted eighth.

vi)   Triplet eighth-note turns in the manner of FD, frequently using the following patterns: *la-sol-mi sol, do-la-sol la, do-sol-la do, do-re-mi do*, the Dorian *do-sol-la me* and the four note *la-do-la-re do*. Sometimes the rhythm consists of four thirty-second notes, the first of which is tied to a previous long note.

vii) Tumbling ornamented scale or arpeggio covering an octave or a tenth, almost always containing blue notes; this frequently occurs in the second phrase of a melody and can be immensely complex.

viii) A dotted quarter note followed by two stepwise descending sixteenth notes returning to the starting pitch *la sol-fa la*, or sometimes *do la-sol do*; this occurs in the Standard Quartet 1894 cylinder recording of *Keep Movin'*.

ix)   An ornament consisting of two sixteenth notes preceding a longer note, The second sixteenth note is a tone below the first, followed by a descending minor third, *la-sol-mi* [or more rarely *me*] with transpositions.

x)   A *sol-la-do (re) mi* ornament at a song's opening.

xi)   Traditional ornaments having a worldwide currency such as passing tones, lower mordents, anticipatory notes and cambiatas decorating a falling or rising fourth.

Afro-American Choral Ensembles

12 Traditional antebellum Afro-American choral singing

The young FD would have heard a number of different ensembles. From passing riverboats he would have heard snatches of male solo singing, particularly riverboat-soundings, possibly call and response work songs, and male ensemble [Quartet] songs. His plantation workers at Solano Grove would have sung field-hollers, work songs, songs accompanied by the banjo together with banjo solos and, in the evening, mixed ensemble singing. Coming from neighboring plantation across the St. Johns river he might have heard snatches of mixed ensemble singing in the evenings.32

A note at this time regarding Afro-American choral singing; the earliest styles were those brought from Africa - choral singing there was most often accompanied, but since very few instruments were brought over, choral singing became of necessity *a cappella*. The traditional form was call-and-response; the call was almost always solo, whilst the response was sometimes unison, although organum, upper pedal tones and freely improvised multi-voiced tumbling descants were freely employed. Over time the AB structure of the songs changed to ABAB or ABAC thereby becoming strophic in the European ballad or hymn tune form; but the manner of performance remained generally the same. This style, which involved improvising free descants, must have stayed the same until well after the Civil War when it gradually started to disappear. It had all but totally died out by the 1950s. Some very fine recordings of this wonderful music were made however, particularly spirituals found in the Folkways LP *'Been in the Storm so long'*. The use of this style, it should be remembered, was also used by work gangs, by stevedores, plantation workers, and also in the the tobacco stemmeries. Unfortunately, to my knowledge, no written annotations of the performance style exist, since the multiple part improvisation makes the task all but impossible. A very good description of this type of performance comes from the landmark text *Slave Songs of the United States* by Allen, Ware and Garrison (1867) published 17 years before Delius's arrival:

There is no singing in parts as we understand it, and yet no two seem to be singing the same thing; the leading singer starts the words of each verse, often improvising, and others, who 'base' him, as it is called, strike in with the refrain or even join in the solo when the words are familiar. When the 'base' begins the leader often stops, leaving the rest of the words to be guessed at, or it may be they are taken up by one of the other singers. And the 'basers' themselves seem to follow their own whims, beginning where they please, striking an octave above or below [in case they have pitched the tune too high], or hitting some other note that chords, so as to produce the effect of a marvellous complication and variety and yet with the most perfect time and rarely with any discord. And what makes it all the harder to unravel a thread of melody out of this strange network is that they seem not infrequently to strike sounds that cannot be precisely represented by the gamut, and abound in 'slides' from one note to another and turns and cadences not in articulated notes.33

The example given in the appendix is the spiritual, performed in 'Shout' style, *Lay Down, Body* [1] notated in order to give the reader some idea of this effect. It was notated from the Folkways recording *Been in the Storm So Long*. It should be borne in mind that the solo part varies for each verse; I have given one example of this variation. The bass part stays roughly the same throughout. It should be remembered that there are at least ten women improvising the free descant parts at these moments; I have given two possible realizations. The singers dance slowly in a circle with a slow accelerando, and at a point two-thirds of the way through there is suddenly an increase in tempo accompanied by rhythmic clapping.

13 The Revivalist and Jubilee styles

After the Civil War, missionaries from Northern churches came to 'convert' the emancipated slaves to White-American religious practices; the Baptist Church was particularly successful, probably due more to the fact that each individual church was totally independent and therefore free of white supervision.34 Evangelistic hymn-book salesmen were definitely part of a growth industry. In the earliest days the singing of spirituals was not encouraged, although much later Afro-American Hymnals were printed. To many Afro-American writers at the time, it seemed that spirituals were about to disappear, but the success of groups like the Fisk Jubilee Singers, using traditional spirituals and the newer Jubilee Songs arranged with white-style part-writing, saved the day. But there is no doubt as to the effect the Revivalist Hymns had on Afro-American congregations. Even today these mid-Victorian hymns have a powerful hold on most Afro-American and Afro-Caribbean churchgoers. The result of all this being that the old antebellum style of singing gradually disappeared.

14 The Male Quartet

A third style of singing is thought to have made its appearance in the 1880s or even earlier, namely the Afro-American Male Quartet with its offshoot the Barbershop Quartet.35 Male catch singing had always been a popular pastime among the educated white Americans; it should be remembered that the *Star-Spangled Banner* melody was an English catch, and that this style of singing probably continued until well into the 19th century.36 Judging from Lydia Parrish's *Slave Songs of the Georgia Sea Islands* this style was also favored by black field hands on large plantations. Quartet singing took a large step forward in popularity in the 1840s when four-part male ensembles became the standard performance group of the blackfaced minstrel shows. Another impetus to quartet singing came with the advent of the large stern-wheeled river boats; boat owners found that Afro-American male quartets were a big draw and their services were much sought after; [37 also becoming popular at this time was the offshoot, the Street Corner Quartets which in turn evolved into the modern barbershop quartet.38 Many recordings made in the 1890s and early1900s featured both Black and White American groups. This was the favored method of singing at the Hampton institute around 1915 when Natalie Cutis Burlin made her important annotations. These unnotated harmonizations were worked out by individual groups beforehand; published copies of Barbershop Quartet scores didn't appear in any quantity until the 1940s.

The move from SATB to male quartet was not a big change since it was general practice to leave the alto, tenor and bass parts as they stood and simply transpose the soprano part down an octave into the tenor/baritone range. In this respect the minstrel groups and the Afro-American quartets differed since the melodic part in minstrel groups was normally the highest part, but with Afro-American and barbershop groups it was the second voice which had the melody. James Weldon Johnson speaks glowingly of his boyhood days in Jacksonville in the 1880s where each hotel had at least two black male quartets, and each steamer and barber shop could boast of at least one; it is obviously this type of singing that FD alluded to when speaking of the Revellers in 1928.39 FD would have heard all three styles of choral ensemble: the antebellum, the Jubilee and the male quartet while living in Florida and Virginia.

15 FD and Blackfaced Minstrels

It is known that at an early age FD had a liking for minstrel songs; [40 however after residing in Florida among black Americans, it was unlikely that he retained this passion for long: the texts for the most part being so offensive. This element makes the songs unperformable today, more's the pity, since many of them have a certain musical interest and character. Strange as it may seem, Afro-American performers frequently took part in these shows, and Afro-American melodies were often used; the composer and minstrel performer James Bland wrote for the genre and the melodies composed by white American composers, such as Stephen Foster were often inspired by Afro-American models.41 These songs were frequently written or arranged for vocal quartet [TTBB]. The Minstrels had a strong influence in the progress of popular music both in the USA and in England, and, in an unintentional way, promoted the concept that Afro-American music and performers were synonymous with entertainment. The influence however worked both ways.

At one time I thought it possible that FD may have used fragments of minstrel melodies, but after studying these songs I believe this not to be the case. Minstrel tunes have a few characteristics in common with Afro-American songs but not many. Minstrel tunes use repeated notes far more often, as suits the 'patter' nature of the idiom, and the melodies are frequently arpeggiations or ornamentation of primary chords, they are never in the minor mode and do not use Afro-American cadential melodic patterns. The strongest influences in these songs appears to come from British folk music and dance, [42 and very often they contain no Afro-American characteristics at all; of course there are exceptions such as Foster's *Oh! Susanna* and *De Camptown Races*. Perhaps the only cross influence between Minstrel and Afro-American Songs were the fiddle and banjo dances frequently used by the Afro-American performers in these entertainments.

Sir Francis Watson mentions the children singing *Shine, shine, Moon*.43 I have been unable to find this particular song: perhaps Sir Francis had made a slip regarding the title. *Shine on me* was a popular spiritual of the time, as were *Shine, shine, I'll meet you in the morning* and *O my little soul's going to shine, shine;* there are also popular songs such as *Shine* by Ford Dabney, whilst the very popular *Shine on Harvest Moon* was not written until about 1908. The word *shine* does not appear in any of the titles in the three volumes of the *Ethiopian Glee Book 1848* or in Brown University's *Old American Songs* or in *Plantation Songs and Jubilee Hymns* published by White, Smith & Co in 1881. The song has apparently slipped between the floorboards of history.

PART THREE / *Harmonic, melodic and rhythmic devices common to both the works of FD and of Afro-American folk music.*

16 *Afro-American influences*

In order to discuss the effect that Afro-American music made on his work, it is important to decide what exactly the young Fritz heard in 1884 and '85. This requires some speculation, since no one thought of asking Elbert Anderson exactly which tunes he played and sung, and what other music FD heard on those magical summer evenings.

It is important to note at the start that there is a considerable variance between the black music of his two residences: Florida and Virginia. Allen Ware and Garrison note that regional styles varied,

Those of Tennessee and Florida are most like the music of the Whites, whereas *contrary to what be expected, the songs from Virginia are the most wild and strange -* [44
(possibly blue notes, flattened sevenths, large leaps, pendulum and tumbling melodies?).

So it appears that Delius, living in both Florida and Virginia, heard music from the two extremes of late 19th-century Afro-American music. The music he heard had other characteristics not found in this text, for example Allen comments on the difficulty of getting the blacks to sing any of the banjo songs of the era imitated by Foster and others during the 1830s & '40s; Delius was more successful, as we shall see in his suite for orchestra *Florida*. It is a pity that none of FD's notes remain from this period, since they would have been of great importance to the musical world generally and to Afro-Americans in particular; next to none of these pieces were collected. Judging from contemporary sources, FD's notes must have been fairly voluminous; [45 in fact at one time he and Percy Grainger hoped to collaborate on a collection of Afro-American songs.46 This was not to be however since these notes have not come down to us, possibly being destroyed by Jelka on his death.

For FD to use many of the typical Afro-American musical devices would have been very difficult, bearing in mind that Verdi, Brahms and Bruckner were still composing, and many of these stylings would be totally unuseable in late 19th-century European music. For example the traditional swing of Afro-American music would be difficult to recapture and to notate, although FD did have a love of compound meters. The blues slide

10

would be incompatible with this late romantic world, although again FD did use this in *Florida* . The rhythmic clapping accompaniment would be out of place if used for any longer than a few measures as would the extended use of call-and-response patterns. This leaves a number of elements which would be unusual, fresh and novel, if introduced into turn of the century art music and would by no means have been incompatible or incongruous. The most frequently encountered would include the use of traditional pentatonic melodies, frequent rhythmic snaps, the general preference for a fairly low choral tessitura and the introduction of individual songs and dances.

17 *Preferred vocal tessituras*

Before moving on to a more detailed study of the specific elements of music, perhaps it would be wise to highlight the most common performance practices found in both Afro-American music as well as the music of FD, for example, the vocal tessitura used by black American singers. In modern Gospel song there appears to be a preference for soloists in the contralto range. Voice production frequently originates from the chest; this contrasts with black singers from the British Caribbean where high light sopranos and tenors are preferred and indeed are far more common. One need only cite the fame of singers such as Marian Anderson, Bessie Smith and Paul Robeson and whereas many fine sopranos do exist, there is no denying the fame of bass and contralto singers.

The effect that this had on the young FD is that he would have had a predilection for alto instruments such as the cor anglais, and there is no denying his inspired use of this instrument whatever the source of inspiration for the particular work happens to be. The melody of the variation theme from *Appalachia* is first sounded on the cor anglais seven measures after cue G in the key of *C* major, and as on most occasions when FD composes what seems to be an Afro-American inspired chorus, then the soprano part tends to be in the alto range. Other examples are to be found at the chorus's entrance at cue 7 of *Sea Drift* to the words *Once Paumanok*, or the coda of the sixth of the *Songs of Sunset* four measures before cue 41 sung to the words *Bloom never again*.

18 *Vertical density*

Another general characteristic found in Afro-American music as well as the works of FD is the preference for a fairly dense harmonic texture. It was noted by early commentators of black music that every available harmony note was sounded when a full Afro-American choir sang spirituals; this is even more true of antebellum style when generally the quantity of pitches sounding in a chord at any one time equalled the number of performers singing and included not only harmony tones but also blue notes and other types of portamenti.

FD's music with its wealth of chromatically altered chords is also very rich in this respect in both his orchestral and choral writing. Three or four voice writing is not the norm. Even with what appears to be simple four-voice writing as in in the choral entrance at cue 2 of *Sea Drift* mentioned above, the opening four-voice writing in the choir has an additional orchestral bass voice together with another part in the oboe and the divisi violin I lower voice, making it a total of six parts in all. FD's bass vocal parts are very often in the baritone range leaving the orchestra to sound the true bass. Even a relative light-hearted trifle such as the a cappella *Midsummer Song* is very often in eight parts as is the final choral variation at cue Cc of *Appalachia*. A similar section at cue 30 of *The Song of the High Hills* where as always the number of voices varies from beat to beat, giving the music its ever changing, kaleidoscopic, impressionistic effect.

19 Husky or raucous tone

These tonal characteristics are very common in 20th- century Afro-American music; one needs only to cite Louis Armstrong's singing or Miles Davis's penchant for trumpet mutes. The two sounds could be equated in Western concert music, firstly with the husky tone of the low flute, and secondly the 'raucous' tone by the sound of the oboe, cor anglais and bass oboe. Of all late romantic composers, FD probably used the double reeds more frequently than most. His partiality for the bass oboe was certainly stronger than other composers - its use in the first *Dance Rhapsody* is typical and very characteristic. Again, this use may not originate from the Florida days, but it certainly is compatible with music from that era.

20 The influence of Afro-American choral singing on the music of FD

Cecil Gray in *Musical Chairs* [47 made an interesting statement regarding the effect that Afro-American choral music had on the musical style of FD, namely that once he had heard the plantation workers in Florida, it was the rapture of this moment that he was perpetually seeking to communicate in all his most characteristic works.

The one element of great importance that Afro-American music gave to FD's work was found in his harmonic palette, particularly in his choral music; that very unique blend of Wagner's *Tristan* and Grieg's nostalgic folk song settings to which I believe should be added the improvised harmony of Black Americans. It is very difficult even now to eliminate from the mind a picture of Afro-American singers when one listens to certain soft passages of FD's unique choral writing, as already mentioned, the chorus's entry in *Seadrift* [2] where we have all of the Afro-American characteristics; these are slow falling chromatic lines in inner voices, usually passing through blue-note complexes, a low tessitura and the obligatory secondary dominant at the cadence. Secondary dominant discords are not a new phenomenon in European music, but his use of them is typically Black as is seen in the final repeated phrase accompanying the words *When the Sun goes down* in his 1890 setting of a Bjørnson text in *Twilight Fancies* [3].

There is a variance of opinion regarding the source of the choral music heard by FD on these tropical evenings. FD in a letter to Elgar in January, 1934, specifically mentions four-part singing from the workers' quarters at the back of the orange grove.48 Another source mentions that FD liked to listen to singing originating from over the water; it should be remembered that the St. Johns river is wide at this point and any music heard from that direction would have been very soft and of a somewhat blurred nature.49   A possible advocate for this reading of the Florida moments can be found in Eileen Southern's *Readings in Black American Music* where a participant in the *Library of Congress Slave Narrative Collection*, James Deane of Baltimore, Maryland, recalls that

*When we wanted to meet at night we had an old conk : we blew that. We all would meet on the bank of the Potomac River and sing across the river to the slaves in Virginia, and they would sing back to us.*50
(The dying embers of an African tradition perhaps?)

Yet another alternative analysis to this discussion could be that the inspirational music could well have come from male vocal groups employed on the riverboats as they journeyed past.51

The songs and spirituals heard from his workers' quarters, at first sight would appear to have been the more modern jubilee style singing with its traditional Western diatonic chording; this is to a certain extent corroborated by Allen, Ware and Garrison in their 1867 *Slave Songs of the United States* who state that European-influenced singing is to be found in Florida whereas the more African-based idioms would have been encountered in Virginia.52 Conflicting with this view is the fact that Peter Warlock describes how FD's teacher and friend Thomas Ward described the music heard by FD as not using the harmony of the hymnbooks but something far richer and which baffled his (Ward's) attempts to analyze it by traditional methods; perhaps bluenotes and liberal portamenti were used as part of the fabric?[53] It would seem that the plantation worker's musicwas something of a hybrid, and not jubilee style music at all. Another possibility is that the music heard from the plantation over the water could well have used the older traditional antebellum idiom. This would be the case if the plantation were larger, since more singers are required in order to get the necessary sliding-cluster effect.

The harmonic influence of the jubilee-style music would have been rather limited, since FD had only a passing interest in traditional chording from a compositional point of view, no matter how well the chords were selected. Should the over-the-water singing have been of the earlier style however, it would have been very difficult, if not impossible, for him to introduce the entire effect into the world of 19th-century European Art-Music; but then the 'impossible' effect of this music heard from a distance might well have intrigued him with its modal or pentatonic melodies accompanied by the cascading free descants consisting mainly of slowly falling portamenti passing through the blue-note scale degrees as illustrated in *Lay down, body* [1].

I think it important to differentiate between the 'moment of realisation' and the harmonic influence that Afro-American traditional singing would later have on his approach to harmony. They are probably two entirely different occurrences possibly separated by a period of time of up to a year or more, namely the original 'moment of realization' at Solano grove, and the sliding chromatic harmonic influence possibly heard in Florida, but certainly later in the Virginia stemmeries.

The consequence of the chromatic antebellum extended 'moment of realization' would have been that which was later to transform his music into the very unique Delian sound to be used in every extended choral work from *Appalachia* on. Attention should be drawn to the fact that at every moment in the final choral variation of *Appalachia*, or in the section already mentioned in *The Song of the High Hills*, at least one voice is singing a descending chromatic scale, and at one point in the former, six voices are singing different descending chromatic lines. I feel that this is as far as any European composer writing at the turn of the 20th century could go in imitating the antebellum choral sound.

Another upshot of the influence of this Afro-American style is the resulting density of the sound where a chord very often contains every available harmony note in the total vertical spectrum together with blue notes and possibly even sevenths and ninths. How often do we hear simple non-chromatic four-part writing in the choral works of FD? Eight voices are the norm. In short the chromatic choral variation at cue Cc of *Appalachia* is the effect of the early antebellum singing style heard at a distance by a very sympathetic and sophisticated listener, modified and arranged for performance for Western European music reading choirs.

Afro-American harmonic influences

21 *Notated and recorded choral harmony from the 1880s and '90s.*

It is normally assumed that FD's very personal harmonic idiom was derived partly from English Victorian hymn-tune composers such as Barnby and Dykes [54 and partly from certain European Art music composers, Grieg and Franck in particular. However it is a long jump indeed from the harmony used in one of FD's favorite Victorian songs, namely Barnby's *Sweet and Low* with its 9-8, 4-3 double appoggiaturas, the i and iv modal borrowings, the V13/vi and the frequent use of vii7/iii, to the sublime harmony found in the second subject of FD's *Violin Sonata III* [5]. It is known that at an early age FD would delight friends by accompanying popular melodies with strings of descending chromatic chords.[55]

When starting this project I assumed that FD's harmony had almost certainly been strongly influenced by Afro-American music for two reasons: firstly since he frequently stated that the blacks had such a fine harmonic sense, [56 and secondly that in modern Gospel and black commercial music it is quite common to hear frequent use of secondary dominant chords, particularly at cadence points. We have three possible avenues open to us to discover if FD would have heard the traditional antebellum chromatic harmony sung by Afro-Americans in Florida and Virginia in the late 1880s. The first source are vocal scores notated at the time, the second very early recordings and the last, statements made by singers in these groups.

A glance through the early notations of spirituals in Thomas Fenner's *Religious Folk Songs of the Negro* [1874], *The Story of the Jubilee Singers including their Songs* [1892], Marshall W. Taylor's *Revival Hymns and Plantation Melodies* [1883], Emily Hallowell's *Calhoun Plantation Songs* [1901], and John W. Work's *American Negro Songs* [1940] was very disappointing, particularly since the Fenner and the Hallowell collections have statements to the effect that the spirituals were notated in all respects from the singing of black singers raised in the aural tradition. Each of the texts shows almost no chromaticism or modulation of any sort let alone use of seventh and ninth chords or even suspensions. What I did find in several texts was the use of 'Modal Borrowing' [a *D flat* major chord or *B flat* minor 6/3 chord] in the *F* major *Listen to the Lambs* [4] and several examples of chromatic neighboring tones, a good example being on the second and fifth notes of *Steal away to Jesus*.

The results of listening to the sound recordings were similar. In the compilation of early Afro-American quartet singing, the CD *Earliest Negro Vocal Quartets*, (1894, 1902, 1910 and 1912), there is no chromaticism whatsoever. However in Vol II a very striking secondary dominant, with a strong cross relation, occurs between the bass and tenor found at the opening of the Dinwiddie Colored Quartet's 1902 recording of *My Way is Cloudy*, i.e., I [*B Flat*+] - IV [*E flat*+] - V/V [*C*+] - I 6/4 - V - I. The effect is very striking, but is not typical of FD's use of chromaticism. In short, the notated harmony used by the Black Americans in printed books of spirituals together with the available sound recordings is either strongly diatonic, or if the melody is modal, then modal harmony is preferred: chromaticism is very much the exception.

22 Remembered harmony as used by Black quartets in the early 1900's

By going down the third track, namely by checking the harmony used by Barbershop or Corner Quartets, a different conclusion could be reached very much at variance with the above results. Several sources have pin-pointed the birth of Barbershop Quartets to Jacksonville, Florida, with the extempore singing of Afro-American male quartets in the 1880s, the time of Delius's sojourn there. It will be recalled that late in life Delius liked to listen to recordings of black male quartets, since it reminded him of his days in Florida.57 It is known that riverboat owners hired Afro-American vocal groups for the enjoyment of the passengers [58; perhaps these were one of the types of music he heard carried over the water, and he did after all reside for a while in Jacksonville. Would it perhaps be beyond the realm of chance that FD had some contact with these groups and that he had an effect on their use of chromaticism and thence on the development of barbershop harmony? It would seem to have been difficult for him not to hear these groups since they were obviously common throughout the Eastern half of the US. Lynn Abbott in *'Play That Barber Shop Chord': A Case for the African-American Origin of Barbershop Harmony* mentions that famed vaudevillian Billy McCain speaking of Kansas City in the late 1880s, said *about every four dark faces you met was a quartet.*59

John W. Work writing in the late 1930s states that the favorite chords used by these singers in the days of his youth were the secondary dominants V7/V, V7/vi, V7/ii and augmented sixth chords. Other chords common to this idiom would include full and half diminished leading-note sevenths used as a secondary dominants and a half diminished supertonic chord (modal borrowing) since they are to be found in early published examples of

Barbershop songs.[60] Exactly how and when these chords were used within a song is open to speculation, but John W. Work gives a Barbershop version of a spiritual *Wasn't that a mighty day!* in the preface to his *American Negro Songs* where he uses the progression I - IV6/4 - V7/V - IV - I6/4 - V - I in the key of *G* major. Later on he gives a traditional SATB diatonic version of the same piece.[61] Work's text was published in 1940, and it is difficult to gauge how much the style had changed over the years since the 1880s; the idiom would appear to be 'dated' by the 1940s.

A check through the chords used in the harmonization of the *Appalachia* theme and the choral variation at cue Ce shows a far wider palette than that used by these early barbershop groups, but there could well have been a very strong influence here. *Appalachia* was written between 1898 and 1903. FD left Florida in 1886, so the spirit rather than the letter would have prevailed.

John W. Work's comments obviously stem from personal experience - the difficulty is finding early arrangements of Barbershop or Street Corner Quartets since there is little to study before the publication in 1925 of Sigmund Spaeth's *Barber Shop Ballads and how to sing them*. The use of chromaticism must have been sporadic judging from the few early recordings we have from the 1880s and '90s. Spaeth's important book gives numerous, and on the whole, simple arrangements of 'favorites' with ways of adding more complex harmony which is most instructive. Generally speaking the most common places he uses chromatic harmony were immediately before a cadence, and when the cadence point had been reached, in order to keep the movement going under a long held note; in fact it is exactly as a modern harmony professor would advise students. It was a long time however before easily obtainable published chromatic versions, totally conceived using Spaeth's methods, began to appear in the 1940s and '50s.

One observation worth making is that as with all styles of music which contain strong counterpoint the rate of chord change in Afro-American music is fairly slow even when the counterpoint is not very active. One need only cite the rate of chord change in 'the blues' as an example. Despite what may be generally assumed, the music of FD is also normally strongly linear as well as vertically conceived.

23 Traditional harmonic analysis of FD's chromatic music

Traditional harmonic analysis of much of FD's music has little real structural purpose since the chromaticism is so complex and linear with the result that the analysis does little to enlighten and clarify the work of the composer. Other than to point to the large proportion of vi7 chords and therefore to the relative importance of the *la* scale degree discussed later in section 43, the accompanying traditional analysis of the opening of the second subject of the first movement of *Violin Sonata III* [5] helps little to explain what is aurally a simple process; namely a simple pentatonic song melody of limited range accompanied by strings of descending tonal or chromatic seventh chords of various types and positions.

Schenkerian analysis would also serve little purpose since the soprano melodic line is paramount in FD's creative process, and the ornamentation and decoration are even more important than with most other composers. (Schenkerian or Layer Analysis is basically a method whereby layers of melodic and harmonic decoration are gradually eliminated from a composition in order to expose the basic structure of the work; it was originally intended for compositions written between approximately 1600 and 1900, the period of common-practice.) It is interesting that FD liked the works of Frederic Chopin, a composer whose main interest, other than the harmonic, lies in the importance of the primary melodic voice.

General Structural Influences

24 Call and response patterns

In so far as the general structural devices that FD might have chosen to use, perhaps the most obviously useful is the venerable call-and-response form as found in the spiritual/work song *I need another witness* [7]. This device is very common throughout African and therefore in early Afro-American music, but it is rarely, if ever, found the works of FD. In fact antiphonal techniques of any sort appear on few occasions. He must have heard this technique used in work songs and spirituals on the plantation and in his visit to the stemmeries in Virginia. The obvious place for the use of any antiphonal effects would be when a soloist is pitted against accompaniment as in a concerto, a sonata or used in an operatic tutti, but there little to be found in his entire output.

The *Piano Concerto* with its accepted use of black stylings would be an obvious place to start, and in fact there is an antiphonal passage using echo devices at the initial statement of the second subject, three measures after cue 3 (*molto tranquillo*) [82]. The theme is constructed of one and two measure phrases sounded between the brass, piano and strings. At the double bar, cue 6, we have a slightly different technique employed when the opening two measures of the first subject are sounded four times, and are answered by upward arpeggios on the piano. This of course is standard fare in European concertos, and it is extremely unlikely that FD considered this a device inspired from his years in Florida. A similar occurrence takes place in the *Violin Concerto* when at *maestoso* two measures after cue 10 and later at *marcato* three measures before cue 31 where brass fanfares are answered by violin arpeggios; statement and answer certainly, but call-and-response? Another possibility is to be found six measures after cue 1: *poco piu animato* in the *Sunset* movement of *Florida*, dotted eighth-note horns responding to the cor anglais solo with the bass clarinet in canon.

One or two measure motivic repetitions are present in abundance in one of FD's most controversial works. In the *Requiem*, for example, the first measure of the opening subject consists of the pitches *E, F# G*; this is repeated and followed by another two-measure phrase. The opening two measures are sounded again, this time answered by a different two-measure phrase. The opening measure is sounded yet again, but this time the theme becomes open-ended and we move on into the piece: structurally antiphonal but not call-and-response. In other words, if FD did use call-and-response patterns. It can always be explained away as being a typical European technique, for example an echo device, or simply an attempt to keep the movement going during a long note at the end of a phrase; if a pattern is repeated, it is simple common-practice style phrase repetition.

It therefore becomes apparent that what really moved FD were the choral textures and melodies heard from the far bank of the St Johns River or from male quartets singing on passing sternwheelers together with Elbert Anderson's secular songs and banjo playing.

25 Improvisation (variation)

The use of improvisation in European Art Music of the late Romantic period was really limited to organists playing in church, or later in the cinema, or in a cadenza section of a concerto. Variation on the other hand is found in almost all cultures, and of course this art or technique was used from the earliest times in both Art and Popular music; it would have been quite simple for a composer to decorate melodies or motives in the Afro-American style. The use of ornamentation in Afro-American music has already been discussed in the *Section 9: Afro-American ornamentation,* and its use in African music, Antebellum Spirituals, Gospel, Blues and Jazz is widely known. To use these techniques in late Romantic music would not have been impossible, since written-out improvisation and variation were obviously perfectly feasible. Take for example that most exceptional passage in the third movement of the *Requiem* where FD gradually changes (develops) a turn from one based on the chromatic scale found at the end of the the second movement to the woodwind and string's searing blue *do-re-fi-re* turn at the climax of the third movement [200].

Regarding ornamentation, it should be remembered that when folk melodies were collected in the 19th century it was totally ignored; in fact the collectors went to great ends to eliminate it in order to find and notate the basic nuclear melody. FD on the other hand did use some ornamentation gathered from the time spent in Florida and Virginia, such as the various turns, blue notes and sixteenth-note ornaments. There is also the question of style; perhaps FD found use of many of the more complex Afro-American devices too obtrusive for European art-music purposes.

26 Close relationship to the dance

The Dance certainly plays an important part of FD's music just as it does in African music. Important examples exist in the two Dance Rhapsodies, the 12/8 *allegretto* finale of the *Violin Concerto*, the *Danza* and the *Calinda* sections of *Florida*, the *Midsummer Song*, the slow gavotte of *To be sung of a summer night on the water*, the waltz-like 6/8 section *andante con grazia* at cue U of *Appalachia*, and the variations from cue 7 to 15 of *Brigg Fair*. There is always an easy grace to these movements which is at variance with the modern perception of Afro-American dance as something exciting, even violent. The use of the triplet 'swing' rhythm in much of the older Black-American dances, songs and spirituals give much of FD's music that same easy feel.

27 'Banjo (m'bira)' and 'River' influenced accompaniments

Perhaps the only instrumental device which FD used and which originated from his years in the US is the use of the banjo as a continuum instrument. This instrument when used in this traditional manner is obviously an m'bira substitute, the banjo being derived by Afro-Americans from an African long necked plucked lute with a skin covered sound box. When this instrument is used in the traditional manner, the rhythm generally consists of a long string of sixteenth notes; this use is also found in white Appalachian country music. A quarter-note melody accompaniment by running sixteenth notes is also a staple of European Art Music found as early as Elizabethan virginal variations and in even earlier instrumental works.

FD's use of it can be found as an accompaniment to the melody found in the *Danza* section of the *Sunset* movement from *Florida* [8]. The sixteenth notes form arpeggios in the cello/viola range and are performed *pizzicato*. The banjo is of course a tenor instrument, sounding in this range and of necessity making much use of close position triadic patterns. Bearing in mind the nature of the first and second violin's melody, I think that FD intended the cellos and violas to imitate the sound of the banjo. Beecham alluded to the Afro-American nature of this section when he wrote

*'Sunset' after a quiet opening drifts into another lively dance, inspired by the kindly remembrance of the Negro friends on the plantations and the vesperal entertainment provided by them for his entertainment.*62

At the dance-like section commencing eleven measures after cue B in *Appalachia* [9], we have another banjo inspired passage; this time the time signature is 12/8 and the harp plays a continuous series of eighth notes in the tenor/alto range with a simplified version omitting the second eighth note in every beat played by pizzicato violas (marcato) and bassoons I & II. After ten measures the effect disappears to be replaced by descending arpeggios in the higher strings and woodwind. As FD's compositional style matured we find detached sixteenth-note counter-melodies gradually moving up into the higher pitch range of the treble clef. Such a refined example can be found in the violin I and II descant at cue 9 of *Brigg Fair* [10], and it occurs frequently throughout much of the work; the instrument performing it is no longer the banjo, but it is a logical growth from the original concept of a detached sixteenth-note accompaniment. An even later example is to be found at the start of the final section of the *Violin Concerto* which commences at cue 32 [11] and which again consists of a stream of high, mostly detached sixteenth notes this time played by the solo violin accompanied by quarter and eighth notes on the flutes and bassoons and by string pizzicato eighth notes punctuating the woodwind voices.

At the other extreme of the sound spectrum, on a number of occasions FD uses high instruments, particularly the violins to play soft legato continuous sixteenth or eighth notes to give an impression of flowing or lapping water as in the middle section of the *Late Swallows* movement of the *String Quartet* [12] or six measures after cue 11 of *In a Summer Garden* [191]; it is possible that FD may have had the St. Johns River in mind when he conceived these sections. Another example can be found in the opening movement of *Florida* seven measures before cue 3 [13] where the concept of 'River' affected the melodic construction. This melody consists mainly of sixteenth notes which outline secondary sevenths and is first played by the oboe and later by the violins and flutes. In the first two measures the vi 7 chord is outlined thereby giving the scale degree *la* more importance than normal in a melody and giving the melody at the same time an Afro-American character which is discussed later in section 43. I feel that it is probable that the St. Johns River was the inspiration for the general effect but that the pitches had their inspiration in the playing of the banjo.

Somewhere in between the legato and the staccato types comes the passage at the opening of the opera *A Village Romeo and Juliet* [14], and as a result this is rather more problematic. The melody has Afro-American elements in it, whilst the arpeggiated triplet eighth notes in the second violins and the violas fall somewhere between these two extremes. Obviously both banjo and Floridian bodies of water couldn't have been further from FD's mind as he wrote this.

Of course banjos play structures other than streams of continuous fast notes; fast melodies using a mixture of sixteenth and eighth notes, or eighths and quarter notes, also sound very effective. The use of notes of longer duration is of course pointless because of the rapid decay inherent to the instrument. If a long note does crop up in a piece then a 'break' is inserted. Sometimes it seems that FD seeks to imitate the music of the banjo, or pizzicato strings, with the human voice. The choral counter melody at the double-bar, cue19, *poco piu mosso ma moderato* in movement three of *A Mass of Life* [15] is an example of this. He uses the syllable *la*, which is normally used either to give an abstract character to the music, or else to give an instrumental quality to the line: the performance indication *leicht* (light or easy) is used. As in a banjo solo, the majority of the line is either in unison or in octaves with an occasional use of two voices just as one would find in a banjo accompaniment.

It is quite probable that a considerable amount of staccato choral music sung to the syllable *la* uses as its point of inspiration a string orchestra's pizzicato. But on the other hand, should a legato melody be added to the general ensemble as in the delightful *Midsummer Song,* then one is bound to consider that the effect sought was possibly that of a solo voice accompanied by a plucked string instrument such as a guitar, harp, lute or banjo.

Afro-American rhythmic influences

28 *Meter*

In so far as meter is concerned, 19th-century Afro-American music shows a marked preference for simple duple and quadruple times, albeit frequently performed in 'swing' time, which roughly translates into 6/8 and 12/8 times. Triple time on the other hand only appears with any degree of frequency in what was originally the French speaking area of Louisiana, [63 it is however very common in the music of the West Coast of Africa. [64 There are however a few notable exceptions to this rule; for example the spirituals *Jordan Mills* [16] and *Gabriel's Trumpet's going to blow* [17] are both in triple time. These two spirituals are very fine by any standards, but the 19th-century Afro-American was obviously not at home singing in this meter since the handful of other triple-time spirituals in existence seem to fall into two groups: those influenced by English triple-time folk ballads such as *Barbara Allen*, while the remainder are obviously imitations of Baptist Revivalist hymns. For the record, spirituals in 5/4 time do exist, for example *Rock Mount Sinai* from Emily Hallowell's collection.

Delius had a very special place for a rather 'laid-back' singsong 6/8 or 6/4 which I believe came from the traditional 'swing' of the music in question. He used it in a manner very different from other composers of the time - for example the very beautiful *Midsummer Song* and sections of the *Cello Concerto,* and of course the *Serenade* from *Hassan*. I see little trace of Afro-American influence in the melody part of *Midsummer Song,* quite the reverse in fact, since any melodic influence in this piece seems to derive from English morris dance. The *Cello Concerto* on the other hand does use many Black-American inspired melodic units; and so as a general rule of thumb, if FD quotes Afro-American phrases they are more likely to be in 2/4 or 4/4, as in the *Danza* section of *Florida* [8] and in the variation theme from *Appalachia* [6].

In his earlier years, FD certainly favored the use of duple meters when writing a dance-inspired piece, particularly at a time when most European composers would have used 3/4. There are many examples, such as the *Danza* [8] and *Calinda* sections of *Florida* and *Koanga*, the dance-like chorus *John say you got to reap when you sow* two measures after cue 12 from Act I of *Koanga* in 6/8, the first *Dance Rhapsody* in 2/4, the *Song before Sunrise* in 6/8, and the *Midsummer Song* also in 6/8. As time passed he used duple time less and less often to evoke the dance; the waltz finally triumphed!

29 The cakewalk rhythm

Syncopation is far more limited in 19th-century Afro-American music than it is in African music or indeed in Afro-Caribbean and Afro-Latino music; this is probably due to the gradual disappearance of the drum and other African instruments generally, the drum being the preserver of the purest type of rhythm. Nevertheless, rhythmic subtleties are far more common in Afro-American music than they are in European-American folk music. Hemiola is not found as much as it is in African music, but on the other hand the various ratios of the cakewalk rhythm (1+2+1) exist in a large proportion of spirituals and secular pieces, as do the use of snaps and various slow and fast appoggiaturas.

The cakewalk is probably the most famous of all the Afro-American rhythmic devices and is found in all time ratios. It is also common in a large proportion of the traditional music of Sub-Saharan Africa. Typical examples would be the well-known spirituals *Swing low, sweet chariot* [69] and *My Lord, what a morning*, or any of Scott Joplin's piano Rags. This characteristic was also seized upon by white composers eager to use Afro-American stylings; e.g., composers of Blackfaced Minstrel shows, sentimental songs with a 'Southern' flavor, or even European art music pieces by composers such as Debussy or Milhaud. Delius also favored this rhythmic cell using it many times throughout his life. Some notable instances of which are found in *A Village Romeo and Juliet,* including the opening theme of the opera [57] and the opening melody from *The Walk to the Paradise Garden* [18]; it is also found in the soaring flute theme five measures after cue 5 *comodo* from the *Idyll* [19]. FD also developed the unit somewhat by replacing the first or last quarter note of the unit with a dotted eighth note and a sixteenth note, or replacing the middle half note with a dotted quarter note and an eighth note, thereby giving it ornamentation. The soprano/tenor choral melody *Pa he said 'Son, you done grieve your Ma's mind'* entering at the climax of the tutti section at cue 26 in Act I of *Koanga* [20], is a typical use of the rhythm in the second measure of the melody; it occurs so naturally that one barely notices it, just as it would in a spiritual.

A rather more problematic development which I believe FD made, either consciously or unconsciously, was the adaption of this basic unit to fit 3/4 time. The exact adaption would be far too complex rhythmically for music of this period [3/4 +11/2 + 3/4] but with a slight adaption 1+2+1 could become 1+11/2+1/2: the result being the basic sarabande rhythm [21]. Like the 2/4 cakewalk rhythm this was much favored by FD; one need only recall one of FD's happiest inspirations; namely the melody at measure 31 of the first movement of *Violin Sonata III* already mentioned [5], or the ornamented version found cue 290 in the final section *piu lento, molto tranquillo* of the *Cello Concerto* [22], or the orchestral theme found one measure after measure 231 in Act II of *Irmelin* [23]. or its use in alternate measures in the tutti section at cue 220 of *A Dance Rhapsody No. 2*. The *Irmelin* theme shares much in common in this respect with motives from the *Cello Sonata* and *Violin Sonata III*, as can be ascertained from composite example 155. This basic sarabande rhythm is found in the early spiritual from Virginia, *Jordan's Mills* [16]. It is not impossible that FD first heard this song whilst residing in Virginia in 1885, it also remotely possible that he encountered the original Spanish-Indian version of the sarabande at first hand whilst in Florida,

30 Triplets and dotted notes

Triplets and dotted notes are very common in both FD's works and in Afro-American music. Regarding triplets one need hardly comment upon this statement since almost every Delian turn (see section 43) involves the use of triplets. I feel that FD's use of triplets in the turns comes as much from Afro-American sources as it does from Grieg's *En Svane* [109], and his penchant for dotted notes probably comes equally as much from his Florida years as it does from his obvious love of the dance. Typical Afro-American use of triplets can be found in the spirituals *Steal away to Jesus* [24] and *Sometimes I feel like a Motherless Child* [25] and in the African counting song collected by Dorothy Scarborough in Louisiana in the early 1920s [26].

FD's use of dotted notes presents more of a problem, since they are so common in his music and their use so varied. To give just three examples of many: the song *I-Brasil* [27] where well over three-quarters of the ever-present quavers are dotted, the first *Dance Rhapsody* whose main subject and codetta phrase consists almost totally of either triplets or dotted notes [41], and the *Air and Dance* [28] where in both movements the melodic line consists largely of dotted quarter notes followed by eighths. This repetitive use of the unit is not found in Afro-American vocal music with any degree of frequency, since it is suited more to instrumental music, however there are at least two examples where the melodic line consists largely of dotted notes, the first is the ballad-like *The Lonesome Road* [29] and the Afro-French American *La Pluie Tombe,* a mosquito song from New Orleans [30]; it is unlikely, but not impossible, that FD would have heard the latter.

31 The Afro-American snap-rhythm

The downbeat snap sixteenth note followed by a dotted eighth note as a unit is found in Afro-American music as well as in the traditional instrumental music of Scotland which had a large currency in the New World, particularly in Appalachian region. I feel that FD's frequent use of the the snap comes primarily from his interest in Afro-American rather than Gaelic music for reasons to be discussed later in section 58. This one-beat unit, like the cakewalk rhythm, is very common in all types of African music, both at cadence points and within phrases. Its appearance in Afro-American music is often preceded by the reverse unit on the upbeat - dotted 1/8 followed by a 1/16 note which I call 'unit X', or equally common, the same unit but double the length; this also appears frequently in FD's music. Typical examples are found in the spirituals *Lay Down Body* [1], *Oh, Religion is a Fortune* [31] and the oarsman song *Lay this Body down* [32] with its very impressive use of the prepared snap. This unprepared snap, however, is much rarer in the music of the Afro-Americans who obviously found it rather too aggressive, but nevertheless it is found in the spiritual *Rise, Mourners* [33]. A fine instance of its Gaelic use can be found in the refrain of the lament *Cumha Aonghuis* [34] from Helen Creighton's *Gaelic Songs in Nova Scotia*. FD's used these units particularly in the principal *D* minor theme at cue 19 in the central slow section of the *Violin Concerto* [35] and in the jaunty *F sharp* minor violin I theme found at measure 48 of *A Song of Summer* [36].

Afro-American melodic influences

32 Anhemitonic Pentatonic Scale

Perhaps the scale which most characterizes Black-American music is the semitoneless pentatonic scale, and it is certainly the easiest to spot. The 19th-century Afro-American often used the seven-note major scale, but because it is so frequently found in White-American and European music, it becomes harder to confirm a Black-American provenance to any melody which could well be even of African origin. FD was obviously drawn to the five-note scale, and as mentioned before, I feel that the most uniquely Delian sound is a pentatonic melody accompanied by slowly descending chromatic harmony, as for example the second subject with the double sarabande rhythm at measure 34 in the first movement of the *Violin Sonata III* already mentioned [5]. The melody is almost totally pentatonic except for two short lower neighbors, an *E sharp* and a *C sharp* which appear once only; the piano accompaniment consists largely of seventh chords. There are many examples of Delian themes in this scale; one other will suffice however - the *d* minor theme at cue 19 in the center section of the *Violin Concerto* [35].

Very often FD would use the pentatonic scale for the opening phrase of a melody and then switch to another scale for the remainder; this is discussed in section 42: *The 'shift' technique*. A typical instance would be from *The Walk to the Paradise Garden* [18] where the opening bassoon and horn melody is continued by the muted cello phrase and which for eleven measures is in the pentatonic scale. This is also found in the opening violin subject of the third movement of *Violin Sonata III* [37]; the opening four measures are pentatonic but the final note of the phrase, *b*, is foreign to this scale. Another shorter example is the opening of the *Piano Concerto* [38] where the first two measures are pentatonic, almost certainly derived from an Afro-American song, the remainder of the theme in the Aeolian mode minus the sixth. The subject which is open-ended ends with a half close.

It should also be pointed out that this scale was used by many white composers from Stephen Foster, through Dvorak, to Jerome Kern and Gershwin to evoke the world of the black American. The *Old Man River* intervals of *sol-la-do* and also that archaic unit *mi-sol-la*, as used in *The Camptown Races*, are of course part of the pentatonic scale.

At this stage, I think it also important to mention that several characteristic melodic phrases common to the Afro-American use of the anhemitonic pentatonic scale are also to be found in the folk and classical music of other cultures. For the example the cadence pattern *la-do* together with the snap rhythm is also found in Hungarian, Scottish, Chinese and Korean music since these cultures also use the scale, but with the possible exception of Scottish music, FD never mentioned any of these national musics as having any influence on his work. Off the record, Korean music also uses 6/8 time with a great degree of frequency; this would have been very convenient when discussing the effect upon FD's work!

33 Mixolydian and other modes

The Mixolydian scale does appear in Afro-American music especially in the blues, but it is not particularly common in spirituals. When the flattened seventh does arise it is more likely to be a momentary modal switch in an otherwise major piece as discussed in section 42. There is no doubt however regarding the modality of the prison song *Gonna leave Big Rock behind* [55] where both the verse and refrain are solidly in this mode.

In John W. Work's *American Negro Songs* [1940] only four of the two hundred and fourteen spirituals and work songs are totally in the Mixolydian mode; I have selected melodies from John W. Work's *American Negro Songs* as examples in this text since much of its contents were not included in Krehbiel's study of scales quoted earlier in section 9. The Dorian scale is even rarer. Only two short hollers found in the Preface are Dorian, while three in the main collection are momentary shifts. However the scale does crop up with some degree of frequency in the work songs, where it is frequently a 'gapped' scale omitting the fourth and seventh. The use of the tritone between the natural sixth and the flattened third is characteristic: the sixth degree is often preceded or followed by the dominant pitch. FD used modes surprisingly frequently, and there is one outstanding example of a Dorian motive which appears a number of times in the *Songs of Sunset* (1906/8), first appearing at *Slower*, three measures before cue 30 [39] and later very tellingly at the cadence of the song four measures after cue 41 - a 'Southern' feel totally pervades this melody.

An alternative reading of this melody can be obtained by contentrating on the theme's first two measures which bear a striking resemblance to a basic motive found in Southern country blues or hollers, particularly one from Florida *I been a bad, bad girl* collected in 1936 [39]. The scale used in these country songs or hollers with no foreign tones added, is often a minor pentatonic but with a flattened dominant pitch: *la do re me sol la*. This scale is uniquely Afro-American. The only Western scale that uses these pitches is the Locrian mode; both are solely of a melodic character since it is impossible to obtain a major or minor triad on the final tone.

There is one fine example of a spiritual totally in the Lydian scale *God is a God* [40] whilst the verse section of another *I am the True Vine* is in this mode. Performance practice ensures that many songs notated in the major scale become Lydian when the dominant is approached from below with a blue note. FD used the sharpened fourth from time to time, as in the main oboe melody at cue 2 in the first *Dance Rhapsody* [41]; he even used as a sharpened lower neighbor to *sol* at a cadence eighteen measures after cue B in the *lento molto* section at the close of the prelude to the *Idyll* [42]. This scale is very common in Norwegian folk music and so the use of the sharpened fourth has the effect of marrying the two cultures. By far and away the most common mode in Work's collection is the Aeolian pentatonic scale [la-do-re-mi-sol-la] which obviously has an African origin.

Some nineteen of the two hundred and fourteen songs listed 'modulate' between two different modes, a modal shift; a typical example of this is *In this Lan'* [43] opening in *E flat* minor for the first three measures, while the remaining thirteen measures are in the tonic major; or for example, a song might open in the major while the second half is in the Mixolydian mode. This practice is probably a leftover from the common African *shift* device discussed later in section 42.

34 *Descending (tumbling) tunes*

Perhaps the oldest type of African, and therefore Afro-American musical shape which we might find in the music of FD, is the tumbling melody. As mentioned previously in section 6, most African melodies tend to favor three patterns; they either tumble, maintain a pendulum shape, or remain fairly static as far as directionality is concerned, moving
around three to six pitches in the manner of the technique used by a player of the m'bira thumb-piano or the xylophone. Sometimes two patterns appear superimposed, as when a solo performer sings a tumbling melody while being accompanied on these instruments by a fast repetitive ostinato accompaniment. The use of one of these three types of melodic shape in a spiritual is generally a sign that the song is older; in other words it uses melodic shapes from the African canon with the possibility of the composition date being in the 18th century or

even earlier. A typical tumbling pentatonic construction can be found in the work-song *Jim Strange Killed Lula* [44].

Descending (tumbling) melodies are therefore far more common in spirituals than they are in the more recent Jubilee Hymns, and they again are more common in Jubilee Hymns than they are in Gospel Hymns; this shape is not typical of European-American folksong structure. As a general rule, if the melodic shape of the song rises and the piece is in triple or compound duple time, then European-American music has had a strong influence, and so a postbellum date of composition is probable.

Of course, if a Delian melody has a falling pattern it doesn't prove that it has an Afro-American origin or inspiration, but if allied with other Afro-American devices then it becomes more probable that this is so. FD wrote many important themes, motives and melodies that have a falling shape many of which have no Afro-American inspiration whatsoever. However I feel that the following examples have a Black American feel to them and so are worthy of consideration.

The obvious place to commence the search would be in the earlier works, particularly those with an American inspiration, since works of FD which have Afro-American characteristics come mostly from his early or later pieces but only rarely in works from his middle years. A very typical example of a tumbling melody from the second subject group is found seven measures after cue 3 in the first movement of *Florida* [45] where the opening of the subject cascades down a tenth in four beats before rising a fourth at the end of the phrase.

Another important theme with tumbling characteristics can be found in another composition with strong Afro-American musical influences, namely *Irmelin*. Found in measure 231 of Act II [23], this very important two-measure pentatonic orchestral motive commencing in the tenor range drops an octave before coalescing with another motive and moving to the lowest voice, then dropping another fifth.

Koanga, as would be expected because of its subject matter, contains much garnered from these early years. Two very important motives appear frequently throughout the work: the first a simple descending pentatonic 'break' probably gathered from the playing of Elbert. It echoes the singing of Palmyra and commences at the 6/8 measure 10 measures after cue 5 in Act I [46] to the words *How far removed my spirit seems from that of master or of slave, and yet no other life I know!* Both the melody of the vocal part and the break have all the characteristics of an improvised African vocal or bowed lute solo and would obviously fit very well in an improvised vocal part over a m'bira accompaniment; its inspiration comes obviously from the African continent rather than Florida. A similar short motive is found near to the close of Act I six measures before cue 29 [47]. It is first played forte by the orchestra and Palmyra enters with the text *Has he been sent by Voodoo (in answer to my prayers to release me from my chains?)*; it is not pentatonic, but is alike in many respects to the motive mentioned above. This motive also has the three lead-in notes acting as an anacrusis with a double escape tone ornament frequently found in other examples from FD.

Perhaps the most purely Afro-American style tumbling melody is found in the *Violin Concerto* dating from FD's middle period, namely the first violin's pentatonic theme found at cue 19 [35] with each measure beginning with a downward falling snap. The melody has been previously ushered in by the flute and by the solo violin nine measures earlier at cue 18; this theme which has so much Afro-Americaness about it is certainly one of FD's finest melodic utterances, and it is also the one that has the most influence from the years spent in Florida.

The opening solo violin theme of this concerto [48] also has a tumbling nature with both of the two measures of the orchestral introduction using the cakewalk rhythm [147]. The solo violin's theme contains two elements which could prove it to be of Floridian inspiration, namely the ornamented cakewalk rhythm of the second measure and the repeated anticipatory *E* at the close of the second measure. It has marked similarities to the opening of the *Piano Concerto*; the opening of both themes appears to be of Afro-American inspiration and both themes are open-ended.[38]

Perhaps FD's most dramatic use of the tumbling phrase is to be found at the close of the first movement of the *String Quartet* [49], a work which has a surprising wealth of Afro-Americaness in it. The phrase drops a twelfth and on the way uses a blue note to ornament the dominant pitch and concludes with that most typical Black American cadential device, the dropping appoggiatura from the mediant to the tonic; obviously this is a composed fragment and not a folk melody, but its inspiration is certainly Afro-American.

35 Pendulum and arch-shaped melodies

It is obviously important to stress the proviso given earlier regarding the universality of certain melodic shapes. Nevertheless if the passage in question from a work of FD is found to contain characteristics encountered in Afro-American music, then Afro-American inspiration is possible, if not probable. To take an example, if a melody is in duple or quadruple time, uses the pentatonic scale, tumbles, and contains rhythmic devices commonly used in Afro-American music, then its presence in this research should be taken seriously.

As with other Afro-American techniques, FD uses these shapes predominantly in his earlier and later works. The more Nordic 'middle period' occurs roughly between the years 1904 and 1920 and includes *A Mass of Life* (1904/5), *Brigg Fair* (1907), *The Song of the High Hills* (1911), *On hearing the First Cuckoo in Spring* (1912), *Eventyr* (1917), and rather surprisingly *Sea Drift* (1904); but even in these works a little Afro-American influence crops up from time to time. There is, though, one work which dates from this period which I believe contains much influence from his American years, namely the *Violin Concerto* (1915).

My interpretation of a pendulum shape is one whose shape is such that it basically repeats a scalar or arpeggiated arch shape. This shape may be a one measure unit, or it may be of considerably longer duration. Perhaps the purest form of pendulum melodies are those which have a static quality with little or no directional pull; this quality is reinforced by the frequent use of the semitoneless pentatonic scale in such patterns. The semitones resolving up or down in the diatonic major scale certainly gives a melody a strong gravitational pull. FD uses a very typical African-style example of this in the first movement of *Florida* at the *tutti*, fourteen measures after cue 4 [13]. The mainly sixteenth-note melody, which made its first appearance seven measures before cue 3 played by the oboe, is now played by the oboes and first violins, while the clarinets, bassoons and cellos play a lower descant in eighth notes. The first measure outlines the submediant seventh chord, while the following measures contain variants of this shape. These are pentatonic and generally not at all typical of Western European Art-Music, since undue prominence is given to the *la* scale degree; this is discussed later in section 43. What makes this melody all the more exceptional is that the pendulum shape occurs six times in the eight-measure melody which interestingly enough closes on the dominant in a very un-'common-practice'-like manner.

In this section, I have also included phrases which use an arch-shaped unit once only, since this is also common in all Black music. It is unlikely that FD would have used such a short phrase as a melodic unit for any length of time, nor for that matter would the Afro-American composers of spirituals or jubilee hymns. Therefore Black-American folk examples of these two patterns are far more likely to be found in music which still had a strong African connection. Namely that repository of African vocal techniques, the work song; and this in fact is the case. There are numerous examples of these songs given at the end of John W. Work's *American Negro Songs* which the reader may wish to consult. I feel it necessary however to give only one example here, namely the first version he gives of the famous work song *John Henry* [50] which contains no fewer than four swings of the pendulum! Sometimes however the pendulum swings only once as in the spiritual *There's a meeting here tonight* [51] with its marked similarity to the motive discussed in the next paragraph; this spiritual together with a number of Delian themes is shown in composite example 202.

These types of melodies are as common in the music of FD as they are in African or Afro-American music. A particularly fine example is the important opening motive from *Irmelin* [52] especially so since the pitches, with one exception, are from the pentatonic scale. In a quite different style is a very vigorous theme from the *La Calinda* section of *Florida* four measures before cue 8 [75] which acts in strong contrast to the movement's main melody. Interestingly enough, apart from this, I can find next to no Afro-American influences in this very popular movement other than the cakewalk rhythm of the accompaniment. Another important arch-shaped melody can be found in *Koanga*, namely the opening of the full ensemble song at cue 26 near the close of Act I with the words *Pa he said 'Son, you done grieve your Ma's mind'* the second phrase of which extends the phrase back to the starting pitch *A flat* [20].

A Village Romeo and Juliet furnishes much of importance in this study, and the present section is no exception. The opening chorus of Scene VI *Dance along* [53] contains two swings of the pendulum in its sixteen measures; the second eight-measure phrase is a variant of the first, but the shape remains essentially the same, the melody is predominantly pentatonic, this scale accounting for ten of the sixteen measures, being yet another example of the 'shift' technique in practice.

A very secular Afro-American melody is the theme of the second movement of *To be sung of a summer night on the water* [54]. The shape of the opening measure is almost a perfect arch, commencing on *A* and moving up to *F sharp* on the half measure and then returning to the *A*, the following measure repeats the first three beats of the first. It is, I feel, no accident that FD choose to give this to a solo tenor throughout the movement - this delightful melody is discussed later in section 57.

36 Inverted arch-shaped melodies

The other variant of this melodic type is the one that first falls and then rises. I have discovered this pattern to be far less common both in the works of FD and in Black-American religious and secular music, yet Afro-American examples do occur, such as the prison song *Gonna leave Big Rock behind* [55] and the verse section of the Christmas spiritual *Go tell it on the Mountain* [56]. Perhaps the most notable example of this shape in the works of FD is the opening theme of *A Village Romeo and Juliet* [57]. It is a four-measure melody played twice by clarinet I and the first violin against an active triplet eighth-note m'bira-style accompaniment played by violin II and the violas. The first two measures descend an octave, while measures three and four rise a fifth; alternate measures contain the slow cakewalk rhythm.

Another example occurs in the opening of the slow movement of the *Piano Concerto*, namely the spiritual-inspired melody whose opening measure with the falling fifth is repeated [58]; the melody continues with a two-measure phrase which has an upper arch shape. The solo cello's *Sing to Mary* theme in the *Double Concerto* at cue 18 [59] contains a similar construction, namely two single-measure inverted arch phrases followed by an answering two-measure arch phrase; the four-measure unit uses the pentatonic scale, and like the melody quoted from the *Piano Concerto*, this theme is the main subject of the central slow movement. This melody which is probably of Floridian origin is shown with other similarly constructed themes in composite music example 202.

37 Melodies using a limited note-set.

This type of melody, one in which the notes repeatedly twist and turn on a few pitches, is far less common in European folk music than it is in the music of Africa. However a surprisingly large body of such melodies does exist in the works of FD; I use the word surprising since one normally associates a soaring line with Late-Romantic composers. However upon reflection the Delian choral sound often uses a fairly simple pentatonic melody of limited range above the falling chromatic harmonies. This type of melody is very common throughout Sub-Saharan Africa and is perhaps inspired by the playing of the m'bira thumb piano which of necessity uses limited pitches. As with other African devices, it is most commonly found in the United States in music which has but little European influence, namely the work song. and very early spirituals. A fine Afro-American example is the song already cited, *John Henry* [50], as is the equally notable call-and-response melody of *Seben Times* [60].

Perhaps the most beautiful example of this type of melody in the works of FD is to be found commencing at measure 15 in the final movement *At Night* of *Florida* [61]. This eight-measure melody is first sounded in four-part harmony by the horns and is followed by a seven-measure answering phrase, probably FD's own. This theme is in 3/4 time and uses the pitches *E, F sharp, A* and *B*; the melodic direction is essentially up a fourth from *E* to *A*,

A second far more brief example is seen in the opening phrase of the first subject of the *Piano Concerto* [38], and despite the phrase's brevity, it has all the necessary fingerprints to fit into this category. The pitches used are again pentatonic *G, B flat, C* and *E flat*. The material is not merely a mechanical repetition; the *B flat* for example is approached from both below and above in its two appearances; this important phrase is frequently cited throughout this study but is covered in far more depth in section 76: *Piano Concerto*. Further interesting insights can also be gathered from a brief study of the composite music example 153.

Another short but structurally important phrase is found at the opening of the *Intermezzo: The Walk to the Paradise Garden* from *A Village Romeo and Juliet* [18]. This Northern opera has already been quoted since it is possible to find much musical influence in it from FD's days in Florida. The opening motive played by the second bassoon and second horn uses the pitches *B flat, C, E flat* and *G*, as does the oboe melody seven measures later. Incidentally this same pitch-set is also used in the opening of the *Piano Concerto* discussed above.

The first three pitches (*B flat, C* and *E flat)* of the bassoon/horn phrase are repeated, and so it would be thought that this would exempt the fragment from consideration, but a closer look will reveal that the repetition varies rhythmically from the original statement. It is worth noting that both the second appearance of this two-measure motive played by the first horn and the cor anglais in measures three and four, as well as the oboe's version at cue 1, use a variant of the opening rhythm. The subtle rhythmic variation of these repetitions supplies an interesting insight into FD's compositional process.

One of FD's most substantial creations, and one which is not mentioned to any great extent in this study, is *A Mass of Life*. Obviously a work with a text from Nietzsche has a very strong Germanic core, but notwithstanding this, there are sections which show strong Floridian influence. One such example is the ritornello-type statement which opens the third movement [97]. The notes used are three pitches from the pentatonic scale *F sharp, G sharp* and *B* [sol, la, do], and the fragment has a somewhat languid sing-song feel to it. Another interesting subject which fits under this heading, and which will also be discussed later, is the choral dance-like melody which first makes its appearance at cue 19 also in the third movement [15]. This slowly evolving melody fills the next forty measures and makes a truncated six-measure appearance shortly before cue 35. The first four measures are again pentatonic, consisting of the pitches *F, G, A, C* and *D*. At first this melody supplies a background counter-melody to the solo tenor with the text commencing: *'Towards thee I bounded: alas! at my bound thou swiftly fleddest and gainst my face serpentined all thy fluttering, wildflowing hair, tonguelike'.*

Perhaps the most unique of Afro-American techniques is the use of blue notes: notes which occur as slow appoggiaturas normally beneath the pitches *mi, sol* and *ti*. These occur in all types of Black-American music, both sacred and secular. Traditionally they involve the use of neutral and microtonal intervals except when played on fixed-pitch instruments when the lower semitone is used. There are of course many lower chromatic appoggiaturas in FD's music, and many of these are European, seemingly derived from the music of Strauss or Wagner. Yet a surprising large number of these appoggiaturas suggest a different point of inspiration. The most purely Afro-American use of the blue note is to be found in the *Danza* section [8] from the *Sunset* movement of *Florida*, where the first and second violins play the *F* major melody, and at the halfway point, a *G sharp* resolves upward to an *A*. This section has already been discussed and will be further discussed in section 57. *Possum up a Gum Tree* and other songs.

As already noted, *Irmelin* contains much influence from the period spent in Florida and Virginia. A common sixteen-measure melody is a rarity in FD's output, and even this is disguised by use of a two-measure interlude and an echo of the closing phrase; it appears at measure 391 of Act III [62]. A one-measure sixteenth note fragment, which FD was to use later in *Songs of Sunset* and *Cynara*, appears as a interpolation in measure two. The text is well worth quoting:

How beautiful and silent all nature lies out there....
And the fragrant perfumes how they sweetly scent the air......
The fields and woods lie blushing in the Sun's last rays
and the night breeze whispers love longing and bliss,
love longing and bliss. 65

I feel that the melody FD added has a strong Afro-American inspiration. In so far as the individual pitches are concerned, I feel that a weighted scale will help: Lower $G = 27.5$ beats, *G sharp* $= 1$ beat, $A = 9.5$, *A sharp* $= 1.5$, *B flat* $= 2$, $B = 9$, $C = 1$, $D = 5.5$, $E = 3$, and high $G = 2$ beats. The melody, excluding the blue notes and *C*, is basically *G major* pentatonic yet FD harmonises the melody with a *C/G* pedal point for 15 of the 22 measures and with an *E/B* for the third line. The effect is very beautiful, turning the blues third into a blues seventh, and at the same time taking away a certain amount of its Afro-Americaness and definitely moving it into the realm of art-music. Its form is typical, being *A, A1, B, A2,* a very traditional structure. Each of the melody's four lines is concerned with the movement from the tonic *G* up to the mediant, flattened or major, nevertheless at the end of line three, the melody moves up from the supertonic through the subdominant to the submediant and on to the upper tonic via a *D* escape tone; this breaks the pentatonic feeling set up in the opening measures. While the resulting climax is the work of a master, it denies a folk origin for the melody. I feel that if one example could be chosen to prove that FD loved and understood the art of his plantation hands, this would be it. Regarding the blues- third, the mediant is flattened in measure two, natural in three, flattened in three, the supertonic is sharpened and natural in seven, natural in nine and ten, and the supertonic is sharpened and the mediant natural in measure 15.

Another rather more unobtrusive illustration from *Irmelin* is the cadence at measure 756 in Act II [63]; the accompaniment consists of a V7 chord over a tonic root whilst the soprano part has a flattened mediant resolving to a supertonic on its way to the tonic.

The Walk to the Paradise Garden contains several examples of the blue note, but perhaps the most moving of which is to be found in the oboe and cor anglais melody four measures after cue 1 [64]. The blue note, a flattened seventh [*D flat*] (which FD writes as a *C sharp*), resolves on to the submediant *C*; it is the perfect use of the device, which FD duplicates in sequence two measures later. The effect is magical and its inherent sadness further enhances the movement's feeling of nostalgia. In order to really grasp its character, I suggest playing the melody without its accompaniment.

Yet another very fine example is found at cue 15 of the *Violin Concerto* [65]: the violin sounds an adaption of the opening subject in *F* major, but the dotted half note after the four sixteenth notes is an *A flat* which resolves upwards to an *A natural*. The closing phrase of the first movement of the *String Quartet* [49] illustrates a particularly forceful use of this device by FD where the blue *A sharp* resolves to the dominant *B* before moving on to a snap final cadence *G* to *E* in that most typical of Afro-American cadential figures; also at the opening of the first violin two-measure melody at measure 36 of the *Cello Concerto* [85], the phrase begins *fi-sol*, and is repeated two measures later. This phrase bears constructional characteristics with many other themes as can be noted in the composite music example 202.

One particularly beautiful and poignant use is found in *Songs of Sunset* four bars before cue 41 [73]. The text is interesting. The soprano soloist sings *'But the flowers of the Soul, for you and for me bloom never again'* and the chorus repeats *'Bloom never again'* a further three times. These pitches are the same used in the *Danza* section of *Florida* (*G sharp* to *A*). The movement between the two pitches occurs four times; I feel this was probably intentional on FD's part, perhaps helping him to remember his sojourn in Florida.

Percy Grainger mentioned that FD told him of the true purpose of his second (1897) visit to Florida, [66 namely to find an old girl friend together with her child which he had possibly sired while living at Solano Grove.67 He was unsuccessful, and I feel that not enough comment has been made of the possible anguish caused by the disappearance of his lover and child; the mother probably feared that he might take the child away. This double loss probably affected him throughout the remainder of his life. One need only cite his ownership of Gauguin's masterpiece *Nevermore*, and the choice of Whitman's *Sea Drift* as a text with its theme of lost love with its poignant close set to the words *We two together no more* to reinforce this hypothesis. Many examples given in this study are to be found at moments in a work where the text speaks of a lover's tryst and the longing for night to come.

39 Repeated notes

It will be noted that the vast majority of traditional Afro-American songs contain a number of repeated notes. They are far more common in the verse sections than in the refrains, because of the the necessity of fitting extra syllables caused by the presence of irregular lines; of additional interest is the fact that the pitch range is likely to be smaller in the verses then in the refrains. Of course repeated notes occur naturally in all types of European music as well, with the possible exception of all bagpipe music, where grace-notes need to be inserted between repeated notes, and to point to all examples of repeated notes as denoting the presence of an Afro-American influence would be absurd. However, as stated above, when found in conjunction with other characteristics their presence could help to strengthen any claim to the phrase's origin. It will be acknowledged that repeated notes were not very common in the primary melodic line of European Late-Romantic orchestral music, where the soaring melos tended to prevail. FD made little use of repeated notes in the foreground melodic voice in the normal course of a composition, yet they do crop up, usually in an important motive or melody with a more restricted vocal range. An exception to this is found in his songs where there is little Afro-American influence, songs such as *Il pleure dans mon coeur* and *The Homeward Way*.

Perhaps the theme used by FD containing most repeated notes would be the variation melody from *Appalachia* [6] where ten pairs of repeated notes appear in the eight measures of the cor anglais's first statement of the theme and twelve pairs in the choral version at cue Cc. Another possible Afro-American melody with multiple repeated notes is the choral song *Now once in a way* at the beginning of Act II of *Koanga* [66] where the melody has eleven pairs of repeated notes in eight measures. Yet another example from *Koanga* with possible Afro-American influence is the chorus part of the climatic *tutti* at cue 26 *Pa, he said, 'Son, you done grieve your Ma's mind'* [20] where we have seven pairs of repeated notes. The short four-measure melody sung to the words *I feel a strange foreboding in my heart; this Voodoo Prince will bring me to my grave* by Palmyra at cue 28 in Act I [67] has five pairs; this melody introduces an important orchestral motive six measures before cue 29 to be discussed later.

Other pertinent examples in order of composition would include:

i)   the *Danza* theme from the *Sunset* movement of *Florida* cue 3 [8],

ii)   the final cadence from *Twilight Fancies* [3],

iii)   the *La, la, la chorus* from the third movement of *A Mass of Life* at cue 19 [15].

iv)   the subject of the central slow section, cue 19, from the *Violin Concerto* [35],

v)   the opening of the solo tenor's melody in the second of *To be sung of a summer night on the water* [54]

vi)   the march theme at m. 48 of *A Song of Summer* [36], and

vii)   the sarabande theme at m. 34 of the first movement of *Violin Sonata III* [5].

There are of course many other examples which point to a foreign origin of the melodies, for example the opening theme of *Summer Evening,* but with the exception of number four listed above, each of these themes contain other Black Floridian elements discussed elsewhere in this study. I have included at this juncture a modified Layer-Analysis breakdown of two well-known spirituals *Ride on, King Jesus* [68] and *Swing low, sweet chariot* [69], since the foreground level corroborates certain assumptions made in the past few sections.

40 *Oscillating seconds and thirds*

Another Afro-American melodic characteristic is the manner in which a melody oscillates between two adjacent pitches or pitches a third apart; this occurs quite frequently in the verse sections of spirituals rather than in the refrains. There are many examples to be found, a typical one being from the spiritual *Gwine Up* [70] from Thomas Fenner's *Religious Folk Songs of the Negro,* 1920 edition, where the interval is repeated four times in the verse section.

FD used this device in the *Piano Concerto* where a two-measure series of oscillating minor thirds occurs in the piano part at cue 3, two measures before the appearance of the second subject [71]; it also appears in the recapitulation this time played by the first violin in the same structural position two measures before cue 24. Even the opening melody [38] of this work is based on the oscillation of the pitches *G* to *B flat,* the eighth note *C* on the first beat of the second measure being an appoggiatura or an accented upper neighboring note.

A similar instance of alternating minor thirds is found in the first violin part of the *String Quartet* in the bridge section of *Late Swallows* before the recapitulation [72], and also in measure 10 of the final movement [77]. A rather more ornamented example but with a strong oscillating feeling would be the melody from the slow section of the *Violin Concerto* [35] already cited, and the opening of the horn melody at measure 15 of the *Night* movement of *Florida* [61]; this latter uses of course a major 2nd, but the effect is the same.

A very moving example of a semitone oscillation between a blue note and its note of resolution, already discussed in section 38 above, is found at the close of the sixth section of *Songs of Sunset* commencing four measures before cue 41[73]. The phrase is in *F* major with a descending and frequently chromatic bass part. The sopranos sing the progression *G sharp* to *A* a total of four times in the phrase's seven measures. This type of oscillation is rare in spirituals but is often found in work songs and the blues and has already been mentioned in section 11 discussing Afro-American ornamentation.

41 Cadence patterns

Percy Grainger was the first to point out that the closing cadence of the variation theme of the first *Dance Rhapsody* [74] had a distinctly Afro-American feel to it [68. This is further confirmed by a quick glance at the comparative grouping of cadences in example 119a. In fact many of Delius's melodies have this characteristic, such as the *When the sun goes down* closing of the song *Twilight Fancies* of 1890 [3], the cadences found in the themes from *Appalachia*, the *Late Swallows* movement from the *String Quartet*, and the *Dance* from *North Country Sketches*; these cadences are one of the more easily recognizable fingerprints of Afro-American music.

In contrast to the common *re-do, ti-do* and *sol-do* patterns found in Western European music (each being derived from the underlying dominant-tonic cadence), African music frequently uses the anhemitonic pentatonic and so the *V-I* chord progression is not possible, and so *mi-do* or *la-do*, or if the scale permits, *te-do* are preferred. These patterns were retained in the New World and are frequently used even when the Western diatonic major scale is used. *Mi-do* is slightly the more common of the two. For example in *American Negro Songs* of John W. Work, 46 of the 214 songs (21%) use *mi-do* in the final cadence, while *la-do* is found in 33 songs (15%); both of these patterns are more common among the secular and work songs than they are in the spirituals, proving their greater age. It is perhaps surprising that the percentages are so low considering the very frequent use by white composers eager to give an Afro-American flavor to their pieces. In my own collection of field-hollers, 16 of the 63 hollers use *mi-do* (25%) while 13 utilize *la-do* (20%). The hollers use this cadence pattern more often due, no doubt to the fact that these cries have had less European influence and were invariably unharmonized.

While looking for these patterns in the music of FD, one is struck by the comparative rarity of any kind of formal cadence in his music, particularly in the more extended works. FD being a child of his time, preferred the romantic 'open-ended' style of composition - one section moving effortlessly into the next without the formality and the sectionalyzing effect of a cadence. However I have found some fifty cadences which use these two melodic patterns. 66% utilized the *la-do* pattern, while the remainder used *mi-do*.

Another melodic cadence favored by FD is found in the placing of *mi* as the final soprano pitch being preceded by either *do, re, sol* or *la*. There are very few cadences of this type found in Afro-American songs however; far more common, particularly in earlier songs, is the use of *sol* as the final melodic note - often a dominant harmony is implied. Mention should be made of the beautiful spiritual *Jordan's Mills* [16] already referred to which, like the *Serenade* from *Hassan*, uses *mi* as the final melodic note; see the pairing of these two cadences in example 93. FD used a number of other very interesting cadential structures which didn't use these two Afro-American patterns, such as *mi (me) -sol*, and perhaps the most beautiful, *fi-sol*. It is interesting that in FD's only setting of an English folk song, *Brigg Fair*, he (and Grainger) should select one with the very un-English *me-do* cadence. If ever one were to doubt the genius of FD as a composer, I would recommend studying the variety of his cadences scarcely any two of which are similar in all respects.

An additional characteristic Afro-American cadence which FD used, particularly at the end of a motive or melody, is the use of an appoggiatura either short (sixteenth or eighth note) or long (half note) on the final melodic tone. This is very prevalent in spirituals, sometimes being as a result of word-setting as in *'river'*, or *'morning'*, but more frequently as a result of intense emotion using a single syllable. The pitches normally used are *mi (me)-do* and are particularly common in riverboat and work songs; a comparative grouping of three of the *me-do* cademces is seen in example 208. FD used such patterns frequently; memorable examples can be found at the following:

i)   the mid-point cadence six measures after cue 3 *Danza* from *Florida* [8],

ii)   the mid-point cadence of the march theme from *Song of Summer* [36],

iii)   the numerous phrase-endings in the theme from the slow movement of the *Violin Concerto* at cue 19 [35],

iv)   the particularly beautiful 'seagull' motive in measures 5 and 6 of *A Song of Summer* [105], and

v)   two examples from the *String Quartet;* the closing of the first movement [49] and the phrase-ending of the opening motive in the second movement [206].

This cadence pattern even appears in the piano introduction to the song *I-Brasil* [27] with the text by Fiona Macleod. The very frequent 'snaps' give a highland Scottish feel, but the handling of them is often Afro-American. This will be discussed in detail later in *Section 58 - Group II: Anacrusis/snap tunes.*

42   The 'shift' technique

One African melodic device which probably needs some explanation is that which is also found in earlier types of Afro-American music, namely the *shift*. A song for example may use only the pitches *E, A & B* for a number of measures and then switch to *F, G & A* before finishing with *D, F, & A*; see the song *Ta^a-vo na le-gba, yi-ye* found in J. H. Kwabena Nketia's *The Music of Africa.*[69] In our theoretical system the complete scale would be a Dorian mode omitting the seventh, but in African usage this device frequently avoids the melodic use of the semitone, in this case *E* to *F*. Its use obviously gives contrast to a melody, even a mild sense of modulation without changing the overall scale used; a more detailed discussion of this technique is to be found in chapter 14 of J. H. Kwabena Nketia's text. Characteristic Black-American examples using this device can be found in the worksongs *Got No Money* [78] and the road-gang song *Pick 'em up* [79] as well as in the lullaby *O Mother Glasco* [80].

It is doubtful that FD had knowledge of the Afro-American use of this African compositional technique, but it seems that he sensed its existence since it does occur with some frequency in his melodies or in sections which I believe to be of Afro-American origin or inspiration. Like many other Afro-American techniques found in the works of FD, even if their presence was not used intentionally by the composer, it does show that he and these Afro-American devices were structurally compatible. A classic example of the *shift* technique is found at cue 14 in the slower central section of the *Violin Concerto* [129] where each time the opening two-measure phrase appears it is followed by a different note-set. If FD allows the the theme to appear in its entirety, then I feel that it is the version at cue 19 already cited [35] where the melody is played by the first violin section with the solo violin playing a descant against it and where after the repetition of the opening phrase has been made, every two measures a *shift* occurs with a new set of mainly pentatonic pitches: *G, F* and *D*, then *A, F, D* and *C*, followed by *C, A, G* and *D* and finally *A, F, E* and *D*.

Perhaps the best known example of the use of the *shift* is in the variation theme from *Appalachia* [6]; the first six measures utilize only the pitches of the *C* major triad before adding the other two pitches to complete the pentatonic scale in measure seven. Other typical uses of this device can be found in the chorus *Dance along* from the opening of Scene VI of a *Village Romeo and Juliet* [53] which uses a similar effect shifting every 2 bars, measures 1 and 5 being repeated.

A later work which has a subtle Black-American feel to it is the *Cello Concerto*; I say subtle since so much of the work is in triple or compound time which precludes the use of actual Afro-American melodic quotes. It should be remembered however that compound time is very common in African music as well as in Afro-

American songs from Louisiana; one should also note that in the 1880s FD might still have had contact with older former slaves who were born and raised in Africa. The melodic devices found in this concerto frequently have many Afro-American stylings; for example the 6/4 theme played by the strings in measure 93 [81] uses a pentatonic set. The first two measures repeat the same four pitches before changing to a totally different key and then return to the original set transposed.

The melody which makes its appearance at *Slow* cue 18 in the *Double Concerto* [59] played by the solo cello is, according to Gloria Jahoda in her *The Road to Samarkand*, a Floridian folk hymn *Sing to Mary*, and it certainly has many characteristics of both White or Black 'Southern' music.70 The opening phrase uses the pitches *B, A, G* and *E;* this measure is then repeated. The following two-measure phrase adds *D* to complete the pentatonic set. Each time these measures are stated, four times in all, the music which follows then *shifts* to a different pitch set. FD also made use of this technique in another section of the slow movement of the *Violin Concerto* [35] pointing to the fact that this is the ideal tool for a composer wishing to utilize open-ended techniques. There are other examples to be found in FD's output.

43 *The importance of 'la'*

The melodic linking together of *sol* with *la* and the relative importance given to *la* generally is a very important characteristic of 18th- and 19th-century Afro-American melody; it is also a characteristic found in many of FD's motives. The fact that *la* became so important particularly in songs of the antebellum period is the result of the prevalence of pentatonic melody in African music. As time passed and African influence waned, to be replaced by European pitch preferences, so the importance of *la* also waned. A glance at the 20th-century phenomenon of Gospel Music will show that the structural importance of *la* has all but disappeared from the palette, and if it is used, it is handled in a traditional European-American manner.

A typical opening found in spirituals and worksongs is the pattern coupling *sol* and *la* at the opening of a phrase as in *sol-la*, or *la-sol*, or *sol-la do*. In European style melody, it is likely that if the opening note is *sol* then the chances are that the melody would then move straight to *do*, possibly via *ti*. In Afro-American music, this is obviously thought to be rather abrupt; the upward jump of the fourth needs softening with the escape tone *la*. FD's use of this note pattern is found most often in his earlier works, particularly *Florida, Koanga*, the *Piano Concerto*, and *A Village Romeo and Juliet* as well as in a few later works such as the *Cello Concerto*.

To quote a few examples:

i)   the opening of the *Danza* theme from the *Sunset* movement of *Florida, (sol-la-do)* [8],

ii)   the spiritual style melody from the *Night* movement commencing at measure 15 *(la-sol, la-sol-do)* [61],

iii) the horn/bassoon opening of *The Walk to the Paradise Garden (sol-la-do, sol-la-do)* [18],

iv)   the opening of the second subject found three measures after cue 3 of the *Piano Concerto (sol-la-sol)* [82],

v)   the opening of the cello subject of the final movement of the *String Quartet*, four measures before cue 3 *(sol-la-la-do)* [83]

vi)   the theme played by the first violins at *Lento* in measure 93 of the *Cello Concerto* (la-sol-mi-re) [81].

Many of FD's shorter motives contain an unusual 'weighting' of the pitch *la*, and the resulting coupling of the pitches *sol-la* give many of his themes or motives an Afro-American feel. A simple test shows the importance of this pitch in the following: the work song *Screw this Cotton* [86], the reel *Short'nin' Bread* [87] and the traditional spiritual *Ride on, King Jesus* [68].

	do	re	mi	fa	sol	la	ti	
Screw this Cotton [86]	10	1	6	-	5	4	-	[1 = eighth note]
Short'nin' Bread (chorus) [87]	10	2	4	-	4	12	-	[1 = eighth note]
Ride on, King Jesus (chorus) [68]	16 1/2	1 1/2	1	-	3	5 1/2	-	[1 = quarter note]
Take my Hand (Gospel Hymn - T.A.Dorsey)	16	9 3/4	8	1	11	2	-	[1 = quarter note]
God save the Queen/America	11	6	9	7 1/2	5 1/2	1/2	2 1/2	[1 = quarter note]

The following four examples from the works of FD also amply illustrate this weighting effect which is found throughout his output, but mainly, as before, in works of the early and later years.

i) the oboe melody seven measures before cue 3 from the *Daybreak* movement of *Florida* outlining vi7 chord: metrical weight being given to *sol* on beat one and to *la* a seventh lower on beat two [13],

ii) the motive sung to the words *Vagabonds are we* found in the final scene of *A Village Romeo and Juliet* at cue 84 *(mi-sol-sol, mi-la-sol)* [88],

iii) the opening chorus to Scene VI of *A Village Romeo and Juliet* sung to the words *Dance along, dance along. (sol-mi-la, sol-mi la)* [53],

iv) the first violin and cello motive found in measure 158 of the *Cello Concerto*, the phrase being repeated eleven measures later up an eleventh *(sol la, re-do-la sol la)* [89].

Of all the later works *The Songs of Farewell* makes most use of this effect which is discussed further in section 105: *Songs of Farewell*. As already stated, it is this dwelling on the pitch *la* which gives FD's music much of its Afro-American feel without the need to incorporate actual Black-American melodies or motives into the score. In his later years FD's use of this scale degree increased to such an extent that it came even to dominate his use of the tonic chord as in this late choral and orchestral work. The addition of *la* and later *re* to a sustained final tonic chord almost became obligatory at this time, so much so that it entered the general music style of the times both in Western Art music and in Jazz. The addition of these two extra scale degrees to a tonic major chord meant that all five pitches of the pentatonic scale were present, the result being the chord with the added second and sixth; as mentioned earlier, for further discussion of this phenomenon see section 105.

44 The falling sixth: sol-la-do

An interesting variant of the upward moving *sol-la-do* motive in Afro-American music is one where instead of the *la* moving up a minor third to *do*, it falls a major sixth; this interval is far more common than the descending fifth. Truly typical examples are seen at the opening of the spiritual *Nobody knows the Trouble I've seen* [90] or *Great Day* [91]. As can be deduced from the latter song, the basic movement is down a fifth but the escape tone D turns the interval into a major sixth giving it a typical Afro-American feel. This interval, however, does not occur with any degree of frequency in the melody voice of FD's works; yet one interesting example is found, this time transposed to *re-mi-sol*, in the *Florida/Koanga/Late Swallows* composite themes [177-9] which are discussed later in section 68.

Other than this, the only truly convincing examples of its use are found in the opening phrase of Rangwan's entry four measures before cue 10 in Act III of *Koanga* to the words *Voodoo hear!* [84] and in the oboe's opening phrase of the composite melody at the final cadence in the Epilogue [94]. The remaining example is seen in the *String Quartet* [92] near the close of the final movement, one measure after cue 21, where we have the pitches quarter-note *D sharp*, eighth-notes *C sharp* and *D sharp* followed by a drop to *F sharp*; the measure is repeated as an echo. Here we have the typical Afro-American use of the leap, the *D sharp* being preceded by the *C sharp*. Occasionally a downward leap of a major sixth is filled-in, as in the *Serenade* from *Hassan* [93]; in this instance the spirit rather than the letter prevails. The link between these themes and *Great Day* can be clearly seen in the comparative example 84.

45 A held note followed by multiple short notes.

This interesting fingerprint frequently seen in the compositions of FD appears to be derived from field-hollers, street cries, and eventually the blues which FD could have heard at any of the ports of call in the US or even for that matter in the street cries of London or Bradford. This musical gesture is very much part and parcel of the parlando-rubato genre of melody which originates back into the hoary past of mankind. These cries frequently open with a long held note followed (or preceded) by two or more fast notes. Classic examples of Afro-American use of this type of ornamentation are seen in the two hollers [95 & 96] from Willis Laurence James's *The Romance of the Negro Folk Cry in America.*[71]

Typical Delian examples would include the following:

i)   the ritornello from the opening of movement III of *A Mass of Life* [97],

ii)   the flute/oboe turn in measure 24 of *A Song of Summer* [98],

iii)   the oboe arabesques at *In tempo*, three measures after cue 23 in *Song of the High Hills* [99],

iv)   the numerous flute arabesques at the opening of *Brigg Fair* [100], and

v)   the *Marching through Georgia* themes found in the *Sunset* movement of *Florida* [177], in Act I of *Koanga* [178], and the *Late Swallows* movement of the *String Quartet* [179]. These are discussed later in section 68.

46 A held note preceded by multiple short notes.

This variant is even more common than the previous type in FD's work; there is scarcely a single work without at least one example of this ornament. Whether they are all the result of Afro-American influence is of course open to conjecture; other possible influential sources could include birdsong or the pastoral music of Grieg, Wagner or Debussy. Typical Afro-American use of this ornament is found in the opening of the song *Roberta, let your hair grow long* [101] collected by Bruce Jackson and published in his *Wake up Dead man*. Another fine instance of its use is the *Cry of the Buttermilk Man* [102] found in *Mellows: A chronicle of Unknown Singers* by R. Emmet Kennedy. The opening beat could easily have been notated as triplet eighth notes, in which case it would have a strong resemblance to one of the Delian triplet turns to be discussed in sections 49-53. There are numerous examples found throughout FD's works; the most characteristic examples would include the following:

i)   the oboe's turn at cue 3 after the chorus's entry in *Sea Drift* [103],

ii)   the flute's soaring triplet phrase five measures after cue 5 in the *Idyll* [19],

iii)   the solo cello's opening two-measure theme of the *Intermezzo* from *Hassan* [131],

iv)   the solo cello's theme at cue 290 in the *Cello Concerto* [22],

v)   the cello/bass opening of *A Song of Summer* [104],

vi)   the 'seagull' motive played by the flute in measure five of *A Song of Summer* [105], and

vii)   the violin's phrase containing three turns at *piu tranquillo e piu lento* of *Violin Sonata I* [106].

47   Riverboat soundings

Another type of cry which FD would have heard every day and night, other than field-hollers, would have been the 'soundings' shouted by the 'leadsman' standing on the prow of a stern-wheeler with a lead on the end of a rope marked with knots every half fathom.72 Soundings would have been called out every hundred feet or so at shallow stretches of the river. Each leadsman had his own melodic phrase for each depth, but very often these were handed down from his predecessor. Typical examples are taken from the singing of three leadsmen collected by Mary Wheeler in her *Steamboatin' Days* [107 & 108]; the effect of hearing these soundings approaching and receding must have been very beautiful when heard at night. I believe that it is from hearing these soundings, field-hollers and possibly birdsong in Florida that the young FD would have first conceived the unique idea of displaying his triplet turns or cries in relief against nature's sound continuum.

PART FOUR / *Different categories of Delian motives and melodies.*

48   Delian triplet turns

These tend to be short, one-measure phrases consisting of a long held note preceded, or followed, by a triplet turn; they are frequently used in the manner of an interpolated bird or horn call. Gloria Jahoda stated that these were echoes of American street cries, and she states that they were assumed by Warlock also to be street cries, field-hollers and boatman's calls from the USA; [73 however, I feel that the origin is in no way so simple. These figures are frequently pentatonic and are used throughout Delius's compositional career being found typically in places of calm and where a warm romantic feeling needed to be evoked.

There are many different patterns used by FD. By far and away the most common fall into two different categories. The first and earlier type consists of the three triplet notes moving upward before returning to the starting note on the next beat; this is often used in more extended melodic units and is most often found in the earlier works while the second type is of a grupetto nature used in short phrases in his more mature works in the manner of a call. In contrast to Gloria Jahoda's statement, many people assume that these patterns had their original inspiration from the music of Grieg whose work Delius greatly respected. I feel that both points of view are to a certain extent true.

In this analysis I have chosen to use the solfeggio scale degrees which appear to be most frequently found for each turn regardless as to the starting degree or the harmonizing chord. For example mention of *mi-sol-la mi* will also include the transpositions *re-mi-sol re*, or *la-do-re la* in the major, or *do-me-fa do, re-fa-sol re, fa-le-te fa*, and *sol-te-do sol* in the natural minor.

49 Delian turn I: mi-sol-la mi

The turn *mi-sol-la mi* with its transposition *re-fa-sol re* is almost certainly inspired by similar patterns found in the piano accompaniment of Grieg's 1867 song *En Svane* [109a]. This turn pattern is first found in FD's music in the opening flute melody of the short orchestral work *Summer Evening* [109b] from the year 1890. In fact the whole opening theme of *Summer Evening* owes so much to the phrase from the *En Svane* even down to the falling appoggiatura at the close of the phrase; the letter may vary but the spirit remains the same. Grieg's *En Svane*-triplet figure is slightly different however, consisting of an arpeggiated second inversion minor triad returning to the second pitch. FD's version consists of an upward jump of a minor third followed by a major second before falling a perfect fourth to return to the first note (*mi-sol-la mi*); this can be clearly seen in examples 109a and 109b.

Similar triplet figures are also found in Grieg's 1901 *Lyric Piece* opus 68 for piano entitled *Evening in the Mountains* [110], but here Grieg employs the patterns in a fast repetitive fashion quite different from FD's manner of use. If one bears in mind the date, it is doubtful if this piece had any effect on the younger composer's work at all.

50 Delian turn II: la-sol-me la

The unit, this time descending, consists of a downward major second followed by a major third, thence returning up an augmented fourth to the starting pitch (*la-sol-me la*). At first sight it seems that this chromatic or Dorian turn originated in Grieg's 1901 lyric piece *Evening in the Mountains* [110] mentioned above if one ignores the date and the obvious stylistic differences, but it should be pointed out that this turn is a Dorian version of the turn most commonly found in Afro-American music and discussed further in section 53. The issue is also somewhat blurred by the fact that FD introduced it into Act II of *Koanga* (1895/7) eight measures before cue 7 [111], being first sung by Palmyra to the words *a man to call my own,* and then echoed by the flute. A later example of its use is found in the opening oboe call in the second measure of the 1912 work *On hearing the first Cuckoo in Spring* [112] which in fact introduces a Norwegian folksong *In Ola Dal!*

51 Delian turn III: sol-la-mi sol or sol-mi-la sol

The third important and possibly the most common of these call-patterns occurs in FD's more mature works, such as:

i)   *Sea Drift*, the oboe's turn at cue 3, after the chorus's initial entry *Once Paumanok* [103],

ii)   *North Country Sketches*, the flute/oboe phrase one measure before cue 5 [113],

iii)   *The Song of the High Hills* [114], a chromatic version *sol-la-me-sol* played by the flute/clarinet/violin II and cello one measure after cue 3, and

iv)   *A Song of Summer* [211], the horn-call in measure 6, one of many examples in this work.

This turn has far more of the gruppetto nature than have the two examples discussed previously, consisting of *sol-la-mi-sol* or the retrograde *sol-mi-la-sol*, both of which have a totally different feel from the Grieg turns. I was struck by the similarity to patterns found in field-hollers of Afro-American field hands; these pieces were used as signals or simply in the manner of a Medieval *jubilus*: a shout of joy. Each holler is totally individual; it is possible to recognize a singer by his song, a kind of signature-tune, and so there must possibly have been millions of different calls sung in the last century and earlier.

I have made a collection of some sixty of these hollers, but of course there is no reason to believe that Delius heard any of these particular utterances. But there is no arguing that the Delian-call is used in the manner of a holler; it is laid against a soft backdrop or sound continuum in an isolated manner. FD probably first came across this particular note pattern in the opening of the most famous Underground Railroad song *Follow the Drinkin' Gourd* [162]. The Underground Railroad was a trail, with friendly lay by points, whereby an escaped slave, travelling by night to avoid detection, would travel north to Canada [or Canaan] and freedom. These songs contained important information which would help the runaway travel the enormous distances involved; Elbert Anderson would certainly have known this particular song.

52 Delian turn IV: sol-la-do la

Another favorite Delian turn is *sol-la-do la* also found in a wide variety of works. The opening three pitches, *sol-la-do* are a very common and characteristic opening of Afro-American songs, as for example in the opening of the spiritual *Can't you live humble?* [117]. This turn should be seriously considered as originating from FD's years in Florida and Virginia, particularly so since these three pitches constitute the opening of many Delian themes or motives which I take to be of Afro-American inspiration or origin. Take for example the opening of the second subject of FD's *Piano Concerto* [82] or the *Danza* theme from *Florida* [8]. Both of which start with these pitches, and both are from works known to contain Afro-American material. The opening measures of these three melodies are combined in example 117 for ease of comparison.

This turn is also tellingly used in *Koanga* at *piu lento e tranquillo* seven measures after cue 13 in Act III [115], also in the *Idyll*, played by the violin I, the oboe and the cor anglais in turn at *piu lento* six measures before cue 7 [116]; and in the third movement of the *Requiem* where it is displayed and developed to the full throughout the complete movement [150] and which has already been discussed in Section 25: *Improvisation*.

It is possible to trace the development of FD's use of these turns from their use in the early *Summer Evening* as part of a melody to the high-art development shown in the third movement of the *Requiem*; the unit also seems to become more Afro-American simply because of the importance given it by the pitch pattern *sol-la-do*. It should also be mentioned that each type of turn utilizes the pitch *la*.

53 Delian turn V: la-sol-mi sol

Perhaps the most common turn in Afro-American music is *la-sol-mi sol* as found in *Steal away to Jesus* [24] and at the close of the chorus of *Can't you live humble?* [117]. I feel that this second song is very important to FD since, as mentioned previously, it also contains the basic note pattern of the opening of the second subject of the *Piano Concerto* [82] as well as the note pattern under discussion. An interesting coincidence about this particular unit is that it is the exact inversion of that given in section 52 above. As a turn, these pitches crop up but rarely in the music of FD. Nevertheless it does appear a number of times in *Koanga* where it is repeated in different time-ratios played by the cello in Act I commencing nine measures after cue 17 [118]. It is preceded by a chromatic version at cue 17 were it uses the pitch *me* instead of *mi*. A more striking use of a transposed version of these pitches (*re-do-la-do*) (not a call however) can be found at the close of the composite melody in *Late Swallows* movement of the *String Quartet,* two measures after cue 5 [119b] with it's marked similarity to other Delian cadences possibly derived from spirituals [119a].

Of interest is the fact that each of the above turns selected, with the exception of the chromatically altered versions, use only major second and minor third intervals in the pitch-set. The difference between *mi-sol-la* and *sol-la-doh* is simply one of order. Another approach is to consider that each diatonic turn has a perfect fourth as the widest interval *mi-la* or *sol-do,* the intervening pitch being either a cambiata *mi-sol-la* or an escape-tone *sol-la-do.* The two chromatically altered turns both widen the perfect fourth interval by a further half-step. From a more recent analytical standpoint, the two basic units are essentially the same since the inversion of *sol-la-do* is *sol-fa-re,* and *re-fa-sol* is a transposition of *mi-sol-la*!

54 *Delian soaring triplet: sol-la-do sol*

This pattern is known to most music lovers because of its use not only in the *The Walk to the Paradise Garden* where it is first played by clarinet I one measure after cue 2 [120] but also throughout the whole opera *A Village Romeo and Juliet.* Its use spans a wide time period since it also appears in the late work *Songs of Farewell* from 1930, appearing in measure four played by the oboe [121]. The pattern consists of an upward arpeggiated triplet eighth-note motion covering an octave using the pitches *sol-la-do sol.* Sir Thomas Beecham thought that it was probably inspired by a cow horn or some such instrument which FD heard on his American travels; [74 Gloria Jahoda gives credence to this by mentioning that a field-horn was used at Solano Grove to call the plantation workers home after a day's work.75 This is very difficult to prove of course, and the pitches with the close intervals at the start and the wide fifth at the top would make it particularly difficult to perform on any such instrument.

Another possibility is that the call imitates a birdsong since we know that these calls were often used as a form of field-holler; for example in Eileen Southern's *Readings in Black American Music*, we have an account given by a former slave Gus Feaster when talking of work songs. He recounts that *In slavery, some holler when dey be in de field like owls: some like crows: and some like pea-fowls.*76 Whatever the origin of this note pattern, I feel that this unit is an extension of the pitches *sol-la-do* so common at the opening of Afro-American songs, and indeed in *The Walk to the Paradise Garden,* the soaring triplet is introduced at cue 1 with these three pitches played by the oboe and echoed by the cor anglais one measure later. Another analytical reasoning would point to the fact that the fourth note is in fact an upper octave transfer which would link the unit to the turns discussed earlier.

A variant of this pattern appears in the contemporary work *Appalachia* where at *Tranquillo* two measures before cue 2 [122] clarinets I & II play a similar soaring triplet but the intervals consist entirely of thirds outlining a minor secondary seventh instead of an octave: *re-fa-la do.* This form also occurs in both ascending and descending forms in measures 4 and 13 of the opening movemnt of *Songs of Farewell* [214]. Another earlier three note variant outlining a minor seventh which then resolves downward with the pitches *mi-sol-re doh* can be found in the 1896 cello *Romance* [123] making its first appearance in measure 5.

The search for similar patterns in traditional spirituals and work songs was not totally unsuccessful; for example the triplet figure spanning a sixth and using the intervals *sol-la-do me* is found in the field-holler quoted by John W. Work [124] in the introduction to his *American Negro Songs.* Another variant also covering a sixth, *do-mi-sol la,* the *la* resolving down to *sol* as an appoggiatura is quite common; this appoggiatura is also be found in FD's handling of this figure. Typical examples appear in the secular song *Ol' Elder Brown's in town* [125] where the phrase occurs three times twice commencing on the tonic and once transposed up a fourth to the sub-dominant. Other examples are found in two riverboat songs *Woman, Woman, I seen yo' Man* [126] and *Oh, I'm the man* [127]. The first of these is discussed later in sections 76 and 96 regarding the *Piano Concerto* and the *Violin Concerto* - a sign that this was almost certainly one of a number of songs known to FD.

Occasionally he would use two triplet figures in close succession to each other in the same voice to add intensity to a line. An example taken from *Idyll* played by the flute five measures after cue 5 *Comodo* [19] contains two different examples of the Delian triplet figures opening with the soaring figure (*sol-la-do sol*), used also in *A Village Romeo and Juliet*, and followed by the *sol-la-mi sol* type III figure discussed in section 51 above.

55 Sixteenth-note ornaments

Allied to triplet turns is FD's far more passionate use of sixteenth-note ornamentation usually employed in a section consisting mainly of quarter notes. A good example being the solo violin's opening theme of the *Violin Concerto* [48]; the melody descends by step in quarter and half notes, but the dominant has a very powerful ornamentation. These ornaments can sometimes give a somewhat skittish effect, but at other times the result is of the highest passion. The units fall more or less into five general groups:

i) Those which are of a gruppetto nature, as in the horn melody played as a counterpoint to the text *Hither my love, here I am* three measures before cue 22 in *Sea Drift* [128], also at the end of the first measure of the second song *To be sung of a summer night on the water* [54], and in the *Violin Concerto* six measures after cue 14 [129] in the central slower section. It is probably derived from the concerto's opening theme. [See comparative ex. 132a]

ii) Those in which each of the four sixteenth notes moves stepwise in the same direction to resolve also in that direction or else to turn back on itself as in the flute's hovering 'seagull' theme at measure 5 of *A Song of Summer* which starts with a sixteenth-note upward rush [105] or in the clarinet's memorable motive at cue 2 *Poco meno mosso* of the *Idyll* [130]. [See comparative ex. 132b]

iii) Those in which the pitches move in one direction but which employ leaps as well as steps, as in the 3/4 theme at measure 290 of the *Cello Concerto* commencing with a sixteenth-note rush down a sixth, the rest of the phrase being in slower notes [22]. The violin's theme in the slow section of the first *Violin Sonata* [203] and in a similar melody also played by the cello at the opening of the *Intermezzo* from *Hassan* [131]. [See comparative ex. 132c & 208]

iv) Those of a descending chopsticks nature as in the flute solo and the clarinet's echo at the opening of *Brigg Fair* and also at cue 15 *slow and very quietly* [100]. [See comparative ex. 132d]

v) Lastly, those of an angular nature making use of octave transfers or other wide intervals found at the opening solo entry in measure four of the *Violin Concerto* [48] and in the flute's motive near the close of *Dance Rhapsody II*. A very striking orchestral melisma appears in Act Three of *Irmelin* at measure 393 where the text consists of *How beautiful and silent all nature lies out there* used later in *Cynara* and the *Songs of Sunset* [132f]. [See comparative ex. 132e and f]

It would appear that the inspiration for this type of ornamentation could come from any one of three sources: late 19th-century European Art-music, particularly the music of Tchaikovsky; birdsong or birdsong- hollers;[77] or as part of the ornamentation found in Afro-American music. See Section 11: *Afro-American ornamentation*. I feel that it is most likely that groups i, ii and iii listed above could easily come from Afro-American vocal performance practice since such patterns are very common in gospel singing, work songs and field-hollers; good examples can be found in the Jubilee Singers' version of *Were you there?,* the spiritual *I've done what you told me to do* and the lullaby *Pretty little ponies.*

The fourth and fifth groups are slightly different since they are rather difficult to sing, perhaps being inspired by a Floridian bird-song. Strangely enough, these ornaments also appear in work songs, field-hollers as in the *Water Cry* [133 & 208] from *The Romance of the Negro Folk Cry in America* by Willie Laurence James, and even in spirituals as at the start of the third line of the song *There's a Man goin' round takin' names* from *More Mellows* by R. Emmet Kennedy [134]. A very striking example of the sixteenth note downbeat ornament of a soaring nature, possibly editorial but very much in style, is found in *Deep River* [152] from Book I of Johnson and Johnson's *American Negro Spirituals* where we have a staggering upward rush filling an octave; this phrase also furnishes us with a good example of a *do-te-sol* post-apex fall discussed later.

These sixteenth-note ornaments are very prevalent in the solo part of modern Gospel music. It is unfortunate that early notators of Afro-American songs didn't concern themselves with ornamentation. Bruce Jackson's 1972 anthology of Texas prison work-songs *Wake Up Dead Man* is alive with such ornamentation, and it is generally accepted that this form of music has changed little over the years; one or two of these songs even derive from early spirituals such as *I need another witness for my Lord* [7]. Other earlier examples of this ornamentation can be found in Jeff Todd Titon's *Early Downhome Blues* which contains very precise notations of blues recordings made in the 1920s; the style of the original ornamentation has changed surprisingly little over the past seventy or eighty years and so it seems logical to surmise that there was little change in the forty years prior to the recordings.

Of course the *Irmelin/Cynara/Songs of Sunset* melisma previously mentioned [132f] could be totally a Delian invention meant to sound like a birdsong since we note that Peter Warlock drew attention to the fact that Clare Delius mentioned that her brother was peculiarly sensitive to the notes of birdsong.78 It appears to be a two-strata unit and thus can easily be analyzed in two voices: the first three pitches being an *E flat* major accompanying chord whilst the final four pitches (*C, B flat, C* and *E flat*) are a melodic unit with the final *C* and *E flat* completing the upward arpeggiated movement.

56 Tracing themes

I have encountered much difficulty in tracing complete Afro-American melodies incorporated by FD into his works; this was to a certain extent aggravated by the fact that he obviously preferred secular songs and banjo music to the spirituals. Whereas many hundreds of spirituals have come down to us in many slightly differing versions, only a few secular melodies other than work songs were notated at FD's time and only a few fragments of banjo and fiddle melodies have survived of what was, by all accounts, a very strong tradition. The tracing of melodies, which are obviously of Afro-American origin, frequently becomes nearly impossible or at the best rather subjective. However, the task is not as hopeless as it seems at first seems despite the disappearance of FD's notebooks in which he originally jotted down these songs.

As the reader will have already noted, I felt it necessary to place the melodies which I believe to have an Afro-American origin or inspiration through a number of filters in order to make their point of origin more feasible. Should a phrase or melody have only one of these characteristics, then I feel it is not sufficient to claim it as having Black-American inspiration or ancestry. To begin with, I shall concentrate on general melodic shapes which African, Afro-American and certain Delian melodies have in common.

Some melody groupings

57 Group I: Possum up a Gum Tree and other songs

The first of twelve melodic groups to have their inspiration from the period FD spent in Florida and Virginia is that in which a repetition of the tonic pitches on the second and third half-beats is found in the first complete 2/4 measure, the melody then moving up to *mi* at the start of the next measure utilizing the pitches *sol-do-do-re mi*; this *structure* is almost certainly of Afro-American origin.

There are three such melodies in FD's output: the *Danza* section from the *Sunset* movement of *Florida* [8], the tenor solo from the second of the two songs *To be sung of a summer night on the water* [54], and the chorus melody from the third movement of the *Mass of Life* commencing at cue 19 [15] with variants found in *Irmelin*, *The Song of the High Hills*, the *String Quartet* and a very distant relative from *In a Summer Garden*.

The first three melodies mentioned are basically identical. They move from *sol* on the downbeat, jumping up a fourth to *do* on the second half-beat, and then repeat the pitch. Nevertheless there are small differences; the *Mass of Life* example has a two note anacrusis and is in 4/4, while the *Danza* has a single note *sol* anacrusis and doesn't move directly to *sol*, going instead via an escape tone *la*, but to all intents and purposes the three pieces are structurally the same.

The *String Quartet* variant appears in the cello melody in the fourth movement at the double bar commencing with the pattern *sol-la-la-do mi* [83]. Another variant is also found one measure before cue 31 in *The Song of the High Hills* where the chorus has a typical eight-part version of the work's chorale-style theme in true Delian style complete with descending chromaticism accompanying a melody in the natural minor; soprano and tenor soloists enter at the mid-point with a minor variant of the melodic pattern [139] in octaves as a counter melody which has already been heard earlier in the work. Yet another example slightly further removed is the beautiful eight-measure melody which comes at measure 42 in the Prelude to Act III of *Irmelin* [135]; the shape is still there, the opening phrase being repeated as in the other examples, but instead of the *sol-do-do* pattern, we now have *do-sol sol*: a tonal answer! This particular melody is obviously important to FD since he precedes it with a ritenuto and sets a new tempo at its entry.

The last example is from *In a Summer Garden* and is even further removed, being found in the sixteenth-note falling staccato phrase played by the oboe in measure six; *do-te-te-do sol* [136] and other variants such as *do-me-me-te do* and *re-le le-ra do*. This is not the usual sixteenth-note displacement so often found in baroque works, since each beat is self-contained and doesn't phrase-over into the following one. The reader will find a chart displaying the pieces discussed in example 139 of the appendix; each of the phrases is transposed into the key of *F* and transferred to 2/4 time for easy reference.

At first sight there is an obvious similarity to the opening of the well-known hymn *Hark! the Herald Angels Sing* [137]. However this was not to be arranged as a hymn-tune by W. H. Cummings from the music of Mendelssohn until 1840. A little research proves that this melodic fragment was the opening of an immensely popular Afro-American song *Possum up a Gum-Tree* [138 and 139] notated in New York by an English traveller and comedian Charles Mathews in 1822; it was known to have been in existence at least as early as 1817 - its point of origin being thought to be South Carolina.[79] Mathews's notation was published in London in two versions in 1824. It is the misplacement of the normal upbeat anacrusis *sol* to the following down beat and the repeated *do* to the second half-beat which gives the phrase a kind of 'melodic' syncopation effect.

I have found this unit many times in all genres of Afro-American music, the most common being from *Revival Hymns and Plantation Melodies*, a hymnal dating from 1883 where 20 of the total 150 hymns begin in this manner. There are numerous other examples from other texts including a *Cott'n-Pickin' Song* [140] from Florida notated by Natalie Curtis Burlin with a slight variation; it also appeared in 'blackfaced' minstrel show tunes such as *My Old Aunt Sally* [140] from 1843. Another version is to be found in Dorothy Scarborough's collection *On the trail of Negro Folk Songs* of 1923 under the heading *Songs about Animals* and entitled *Charleston Girls* [140]; the opening is identical to the *Possum's* first measure but doesn't rise to the snap, returning to the tonic instead. Ms. Scarborough is of the opinion that the song *seems really a combination of fragments from various Negro folk songs of early origin.*80

Yet another important variant of this melody found in Ms. Scarborough's collection, and one which FD must have known since he used three phrases from it in different works, is the dance song *Hold my mule* [140].

i) Measures one and two contain the opening phrase of the *Danza* section from *Florida* with two small differences. The first is that they do not use the repeated *do* in the first measure; the second *do* is replaced by the escape-tone *la* instead. Another small difference is that the snatch-notes at the close of measure two are eighth notes instead of sixteenths.

ii) The opening five notes of the melody *sol-la-do-re mi* are the nuclear basis for the second subject of the *Piano Concerto* [82 & 140], and

iii) the closing two measures of the song contain the apex unit *la-sol mi* to be discussed later in Group VII melodies in section 65.

As with the Delian examples given in the first half of this section, each of the opening phrases of the folk songs discussed are transposed into the key of *F* for easy reference in musical example 140 in the appendix.

58   Group II Anacrusis/snap tunes

Another common grouping of themes derived from Afro-American music is that in which FD's melodies open with a one or two note anacrusis and complete the phrase with a 'snap' appoggiatura several beats later. Between these two units are normally two to four beats, often in sequence; these melodies are found in 2/4, 6/8 and 4/4 times. Typical examples are found in the *Danza* melody from the *Sunset* movement of *Florida* [8], the cello melody from *molto moderato* commencing at cue J in *Appalachia* [141], the march melody starting at measure 116 *a tempo* from *A Song of Summer* [36], and the slow Trio melody from the second movement of the *Violin Sonata III* [142].

This phrase construction is very common in all types of Black songs, but particularly so in river songs. For example in *Steamboatin' Days*, 28 of the total 69 songs have a snap or short appoggiaturas at the end of the first phrase, while 15 have both the opening anacrusis and the snap cadence. These songs were sung to Mary Wheeler in the early 1940s by 60- to 80-year old retired riverboat-hands who worked the Mississippi between the years 1860 -1880. I realize that the Mississippi river is not the St. Johns, however there would have been similarities and many songs would have been common to both areas. In the earlier 1867 collection of songs by Allen, Ware and Garrison, these devices are not nearly so common.

A typical example of this structure would be the riverboat song *Vicksburg 'round the bend* [143] and the *Cott'n Pickin' Song* [140] already cited from Florida and collected by Natalie Curtis-Burlin in the early 1920s. Mention should also be made of the fact that this first-phrase pattern was most often found in FD's works from the years 1886-1902 and 1929-1930, periods of composition containing the most Afro-American influence.

Of interest also is the fact that the snap at the end of the opening phrase sung to the pitches *mi-sol* is also common to blackfaced minstrel songs and is found, but less frequently, in the songs of Stephen Foster giving proof that these composers saw it as an easily-composed device to add Black character to their songs.

The pattern is less common in West Coast African music, although an interesting variant with a snap at the end of the opening phrase was collected by Thomas Edward Bowdich in 1817; however the melody, *Fantee Air: Oompoochwa*, lacks an anacrusis and is in triple time [144].[81] Notwithstanding this, it seems likely that the figure gained more impetus with the Afro-American's contact with Scottish folk music which of course was very popular in the Eastern USA in the late 18th and early 19th centuries. There are in fact a few spirituals/hymns which are found in both the White-American and Afro-American liturgical traditions: *The Morning Trumpet* [145] is typical; it could in fact have originated in either congregations. There were obviously many contacts between the two races and several early accounts mention the speed with which Afro-Americans were able to reproduce a White-American hymn. On one occasion a Black congregation heard a hymn sung in a White service and the next week they were able to reproduce the same hymn at their own service. Allied to this is the prodigious memories possessed by many 'unlettered' plantation workers. For example in the introduction to his *Befo' de War Spirituals* [1933] E. A. McIlhenny mentions that Becky Elzy sang to him the 120 spirituals in his collection each of which possessed multiple verses![82]

I feel it necessary to give credence to my research into this pattern by giving details of its popularity among the ethnic groups in question by means of the information given below. As can be seen, the presence of these units in both Highland and Lowland Scottish songs was far less than one would expect. Many of the Scottish songs had a snap on the cadential upbeat, instead of the downbeat, and at the end of the second phrase instead of the first. Other songs, not included in this survey, repeated the pitch in the snap; a note pattern not used by FD. A proviso needs to be added to the effect that in several cases the decision as to what constitutes the spirit and nature of a snap was difficult to judge and therefore somewhat subjective and depended to a great extent on the collector's general approach. Bearing in mind these circumstances I settled on the following patterns as fitting the criterion of a snap:

i)   a sixteenth note followed by a dotted eighth note (2/4 or 4/4),
ii)   eighth note followed by a dotted quarter note (4/4),
iii)   two eighth notes followed by a quarter-note rest (4/4),
iv)   two slurred sixteenth notes followed by a dotted quarter note (4/4),
v)   a quarter note followed by a dotted half note (4/4 'soundings'), and
vi)   a slurred on-the-beat acciaccatura followed by a quarter or half note (4/4)

Texts	Area	cadential snap only		anacrusis & snap	
Steamboatin' Days	(Southern Afro-Am c.1860-80)	44/99	(44%)	24/99	(24%)
Slave Songs of the United States	(Afro-Am 1867)	37/136	(27%)	19/136	(14%)
The Story of the Jubilee Singers	(Afro-Am 1892)	33/139	(23%)	17/139	(12%)
Gaelic Songs in Nova Scotia	(Highland Scottish)	16/93	(17%)	10/93	(10%)
77 Stephen Foster Songs	(White-American Parlour Songs)	13/77	(17%)	5/77	(6%)
The Music of Africa	(Ghana 1974)	9/62	(14%)	5/62	(8%)
The Scottish Folksinger	(Lowland Scottish)	12/117	(10%)	9/117	(7%)

59   Group III: Cakewalk rhythm in the first measure of a theme

The cakewalk rhythm (1+2+1) is very common to all types of African and Afro-American music appearing in at least three different time ratios. It occurs in various places within a piece, but it is often found in its simple undecorated form in the first measure, as in the spirituals *Swing low, sweet chariot* [69] and *Nobody knows the trouble I've seen* [90]. From a point of view of pitch, all of Group I: *Possum up a Gum-tree* themes are also derived from this cakewalk rhythmic unit since the pitches on half-beats two and three are the same, but sounded, not tied. There are numerous examples of this basic cakewalk rhythm in FD's output, these being the most typical:

i)   the pentatonic horn-call, one measure before cue 2 in the opening *Daybreak* movement of *Florida* [148],

ii)   the scalar hexatonic clarinet/violin I opening theme of *A Village Romeo and Juliet* [57],

iii)   flutes I and II closing pentatonic elegiac melody at cue 15 of *The Walk to the Paradise Garden* [146],

iv)   a simple use of the pattern is found in the two-measure string introduction at the opening of the *Violin Concerto* [147] using the scale degrees *sol-la-do*,   and

v)   in the *Songs of Farewell* where it appears in the cello's opening pentatonic obbligato figure at the opening of the second song [149].

60   Group IV: Ornamented cakewalk rhythm in the first measure of a theme

Even more common is FD's use of ornamented versions of the basic 1+2+1 rhythmic unit, for example 1/2+1/2 +2+1, or 1/3+1/3+1/3+2+1/2+1/2 or even 1/4+1/4+1/4+1/4+2+1 are often used. A notable example of the first given ornamented variant is found in the *Vagabonds are we* chorus from Scene VI of *A Village Romeo and Juliet* at cue 84 [88]; it is repeated frequently throughout the movement.

The vast majority of 4/4 phrases which contain triplet turns fall into this category, since the turn almost invariably is placed on the downbeat. Two examples already cited should suffice: the flute's two-measure soaring triplet phrase five measures after cue 5 and echoed four times on other instruments in the *Idyll* [19], and the passage commencing one measure before cue 25 of the *Requiem* [150], where the previously 3/4 phrase changes to 4/4, utilizing the cakewalk rhythm as it does so.

A very effective use of the opening sixteenth-note ornamentation of this cell is the solo cello's one measure motive at the start of the *Intermezzo* from *Hassan* [131]; five measures later it blossoms into the clarinet's two measure 'call' complete with a Delian turn using the pitches *sol-la-do* at measure 290. This phrase, with a slight adaption of the opening sixteenth note pitches, is adapted to 3/4 time by simply omitting the final beat of the measure and as such serves as the basis for the closing melody of the *Cello Concerto* [22], a work composed at the same time as the *Intermezzo*. An exceptional call played by the oboe three measures after cue 5 in Scene I of *A Village Romeo and Juliet* [151] is one of the few examples of the the use of rising sixteenth notes in this cell.

The Afro-American use of triplet and quadruplet decoration on the first beat is exceedingly rare, although in practice it would have occurred through the extempore use of ornamentation. On the other hand the double eighth-note ornament is very common, as in the fourth measure of the spiritual *Swing low, sweet chariot* [69]. Regarding the downbeat triplet ornament, a very moving example is found in the spiritual *Steal away to Jesus* [24] which furnishes us with yet another example, although the unit is on the second of a two-measure phrase.

61 Group Va: Ornamented slow cakewalk rhythm in the second measure preceded by a half note and two quarter notes

This 4/4 rhythmic pattern is quite frequently found throughout FD's entire output. The earliest important use of it occurs at measure 613 in Act II of *Irmelin* [153]. An augmented version has already been played by the orchestral bass instruments in measure 76 at the opening of the same Act. This is also of interest since it has a very characteristic eighth-note triplet figure at the end of the cakewalk measure. Another somewhat less important use of this figure appears in *Irmelin* and is found in Act I at measure 331[154]; the first of the two eighth notes is dotted. Perhaps the most memorable example of this pattern is the opening theme of the *Piano Concerto* [38], a most important two-measure unit much discussed throughout this text. The similarity between these themes is clarified in the comparative musical example 153. Yet another similarly constructed theme is the solo violin's opening statement in the *Violin Concerto* [48]. The two eighth notes at the opening of the second measure are replaced by four sixteenth notes, the first and third of which (*G and A*) still dominate the four notes; this has already been discussed in section 55: *Sixteenth-note ornaments.*

The melody at measure 127 of the *Cello Sonata* [155] also uses a slight rhythmic variation in that the two eighth notes have been replaced by triplets; the phrase is of the tumbling variety, and appears to be linked to the 3/2 theme also from *Irmelin* in measure 231 of Act II [23], clearly illustrated in composite examples 155 and 205. Another interesting variant is found in the Dorian motive from the fifth of the *Songs of Sunset* played by the cor anglais three measures before cue 30 [39]. The opening two eighth notes at the start of the second measure have been increased to four by means of an anticipatory note and a lower neighbor; thus the cakewalk concept remains the same since the pitches (*C*) are the same on both beats two and three.

62 Group Vb: Ornamented slow cakewalk rhythm in the second measure preceded by two eighth notes

A variant of this ornamented cakewalk rhythm, this time preceded by two eighth notes, appears at the opening of *A Village Romeo and Juliet* where three measures after cue 1 the cor anglais/bassoons/ horn/viola phrase answers the opening descending theme [156]; on the first beat of this unit we have a fine example of the soaring triplet pattern. Perhaps FD's most beautiful use of this rhythmic unit is found in the chorale-type theme from *The Song of the High Hills* which first appears 7 measures after cue 17 [157]. A case can be made for stating that the melody could well be of Black Floridian or Virginian origin since it is in 4/4, uses the natural minor scale, and the third measure tumbles using the original rhythmic set found in the melody's opening, a common device in African and early Afro-American music. It uses a variant of the final cadence of a very popular Afro-American dance song [192]; this theme is further discussed in section 86: *Song of the High Hills.*

An additional important theme of this type is the second subject of the first movement of the *Cello Sonata* [205]. The phrase is sounded six times by the cello before the piano plays it another three times at various pitch levels commencing at *a tempo piu tranquillo* in measure 45, the soprano voice being doubled by the bass voice at 16' pitch in each repetition. In so far as the pitches are concerned, there is little to link these last two themes except the very memorable rhythmic structure.

63 Group Vc: Ornamented slow cakewalk rhythm in the second measure preceded by various rhythms

There are far more examples of this subsection since there are no fixed rhythmic requirements for the preceding measure. Possibly the most exquisite of which is found in the violin's elegiac introduction to the third movement of the third *Violin Sonata* [37] the piano's introduction of which bears a marked similarity to a theme at measure 127 of the *Cello Sonata* [155]; both have the same melodic shape and rhythmic structure in their first two measures. This can be clearly seen in the composite examples 76, 155 and 205. One other important motive which makes use of triplet eighth notes on the first beat of the second measure is that found in measure 20 of the opening of *Irmelin* [158]; the second measure is repeated four times immediately after leading in to the return of the Prelude's opening theme. The second and third themes from the *Piano Concerto*, namely the horns' and piano's second subject three measures after cue 3 [82] and the piano's *largo* subject at cue 14 [58], are variants since they both have an ornamented cakewalk measure in the third measure instead of the second. There are several melodies written in 3/4 which have the same characteristics, such as is found in the oboe's melody at measure 147 of *Dance Rhapsody No. 2* [160], but their inclusion may be stretching the envelope somewhat.

Again I feel that the Afro-American melody which originally gave birth to all the above themes was the river song *Woman, woman, I seen yo' man* [126] with its marked similarity to the opening theme of the *Piano Concerto* and to the theme of the center section of the *Violin Concerto*; this song also has a fine example of a soaring triplet in the penultimate measure. An additional possible source of inspiration is another riverboat song *I'm goin' up the rivah* [161], while other candidates include the 'underground railroad' song *Follow the Drinkin' Gourd* [162] already quoted where the three eighth notes at the opening of the second measure could have been easily notated as triplets.

Two further examples found in William E. Barton's late 19th-century collection *Hymns of the Slave and the Freedman*, namely *Stand on a sea of glass* [163] and *Big Camp Meeting in the Promised Land* [164]; both appear to come from the time of the Civil War. The former of these two spirituals is combined with themes from *Irmelin*, the *Piano Concerto* and *The Song of the High Hills* in composite example 153 in order best to see their similarities. The pattern under discussion is also found in the well-known spiritual *There is a balm in Gilead* [165] with its elongated anacrusis. The only example found which contains a pair of eighth notes at the end of the first measure and at the opening of measure two is the well known spiritual *Ride on, King Jesus* [68].

64 Group VI: *Irmelin/Koanga/Appalachia theme*

A grouping of three themes with marked similarities is seen in a melody from Act I of *Irmelin* [182 & 166], a chorus from *Koanga* [166] and the variation theme of *Appalachia* [6]. The phrase from *Irmelin* makes its appearance at measure 135 of Act I sung by a Maid to the text *Never was there maid like thee*. It is a twelve-measure melody with an A₁, A₂, A₃, B form and almost seems like an original draft for the *Appalachia* theme but is far more static, never really moving away from the tonic chord in its melodic structure.

The melody from *Koanga* is sung by the chorus near the opening of Act II, 12 measures before cue 3 to the text *He will meet her when the sun goes down*, and then later at cue 8 *He will meet her when the moon is high* and finally near the close of the act, fifteen measures before cue 17 after the *Ballet of Creole Dancers*, *He will win her when the sun goes down*. The shape and rhythm is the same as that of the *Appalachia* version for the first two phrases, but the four repeated notes in the first complete measure is on the third of the chord in the *Koanga* version but on the tonic root in *Appalachia*. In *Koanga* the form of the final cadence differs in each verse with the close of the third version being *re-do-do-la do*, even more Afro-American than *Appalachia's sol-la do-re do*.

[In the Autumn of 2001, Robert Threlfall published an article, discussed in this work's *Preface,* regarding the discovery of a previously unknown manuscript containing several fragments of Afro-American origin including an arrangement by FD of the above melody from *Koanga* entitled a *Negro Song* with a text commencing *I will meet you when the sun goes down*.]

The earliest version, from *Irmelin*, would have been composed between 1890 and 1902, while *Koanga* dates from the years 1895 and 1897, and the final version of *Appalachia* was written between 1898 and 1903. The *Appalachia* version is perhaps a more natural inspiration, but the *Koanga* melody is not without merit. Why exactly FD should use three so similar melodies is open to conjecture; it almost seems that the *Appalachia* version is a growth out of those found in *Irmelin* and *Koanga*. For a comparative grouping of these three melodies see example 166.

65 Group VIIa: *Descending phrase using la-sol-mi after an apex*

There are a number of melodic progressions which give an Afro-American feel to FD's music without its being obvious. Further study points to the presence of characteristic Afro-American descending phrase shapes such as *la-sol-mi* frequently found at the apex of a bow-shaped phrase at the close of an opening phrase in the major key. This note pattern and its transpositions occurred very frequently in FD's earlier works and they were to reappear in later works leading one to suspect that the theme had a Floridian origin. A good example of Afro-American usage can be found in the closing phrase of the folk-song *Hold my Mule* [140] mentioned in section 57. There are many such examples of this to be found, but a particularly fine instance of the transposed form *re-do-la* is found at the opening of the refrain of *Boatman Dance, Boatman Sing* from May Wheeler's collection *Roustabout Songs* [167], a variant of which was also popular as a minstrel song *De Boatman Dance* from the *Ethiopian Glee Book* by 'Gumbo Chaff' of 1848 [168]. As a point of interest, the same opening three-note pattern is found at cue 193 of Act II of *Porgy and Bess* sung to the words *Here come de honey man*; it is known that Gershwin used 'Southern' Afro-American street cries in this section of his opera!

FDs use of this melodic unit is seen at the close of the early song *Twilight Fancies* to the words *When the sun goes down* [3], and in Vrenchen's oft repeated two-measure phrase at cue 6 in Act IV of *A Village Romeo and Juliet* [187]. Another instance can be found in the violin's slow introduction to the final movement of *Violin Sonata III* [37] where the opening rhapsodic violin melody, pentatonic except for the final tone, is repeated up a perfect fifth and later in the closing measures of the work. This subject also shows a marked resemblance to several themes from the *Cello Sonata* and *Irmelin*; the link can be seen clearly in the composite musical examples 155 and 205. As mentioned earlier, Delian-calls frequently utilize the *mi-sol-la* pitches as seen in *Violin Sonata II* where the piano repeats the pitches at the apex of the two measure introduction at *poco meno mosso - piu tranquillo* in the middle of the first movement [169].

66 Group VIIb: *Descending phrase using do-te-sol after an apex*

This transposition of the previous *la-sol-mi* phrase is so common that I have listed it separately. The pattern is to be found predominantly in the natural minor or Mixolydian mode with their flattened leading tones. Fine Delian examples appear in the opening theme of the *Piano Concerto* [38], the opening theme from *Irmelin* [52], the 1930 cello *Elegy's* melody at measure seventeen [221], the piano's opening of the final movement of *Violin Sonata III* [37], and in the fifth measure of the chorale-like melody found in *The Song of the High Hills* [157] already discussed above in section *62*. At first sight it would seem that the example from *Violin Sonata III* employs yet another transposed version (*mi-re-ti)* until one realizes that the movement opens in *E* minor pentatonic before moving smartly to *C* major in measure four.

Irmelin despite its Nordic setting, and like the *Piano Concerto* and the *Third Violin Sonata*, is a work rich in subtle Afro-Americanisms.   In FD's earlier days it is possible that he embraced the concept of using Floridian Afro-American stylings as a way to give his works a distinct identity; these stylings on the whole disappeared from his creations in his middle years only to reappear again at the end of his life, particularly in the *String Quartet*, the *Cello Concerto, A Song of Summer* and *Violin Sonata III*.

Afro-American usage of this note pattern utilizing the subtonic is found at the opening of the work song *Gonna leave Big Rock behind* [55] and in the antiphonal spiritual *I'm agoing to join the Band* [170] both from John W. Work's *American Negro Songs*. For a comparative grouping of the themes discussed in this section see composite example 76.

67   Group VIII: Descending phrase using do-la-sol after an apex

Yet another variant of the above unit is one in which the pitches used after the opening apex of a spiritual or secular song utilizes the tumbling pitches *do-la-sol.* This occurs when both the diatonic major or pentatonic scales are used; it also appears frequently at the start of the verse section of a spiritual. Two fine examples appear in the spiritual *We are climbing Jacob's ladder* [171] where the climatic unit is repeated three times also in the second half of the refrain section of *There's a meeting here tonight* [51] with its marked similarity to the important motive found at the close of the Prelude to Act I of *Irmelin* [172]; this note pattern is found most often in early spirituals probably because of its pentatonic nature. The latter of these two spirituals contains two phrases similar to those found in various compositions of FD; these spirituals together with a number of other thematic phrases are grouped together in the composite example 202 for ease of comparison. There is an obvious link here with the chapters discussing the importance of the *la* pitch in section 43 and the Delian-turn IV considered in section 52 which also uses these three scale degrees.

Though not as common in the music of FD as the *la-sol-mi* pattern, it serves roughly the same purpose, giving a pentatonic tumbling effect to the second half of an arch phrase. The examples are found in the composer's earlier works, particularly in *Irmelin,* which contains two fine examples; the first is from the opera's prelude mentioned in the previous paragraph with the interesting recapitulation, varied of course, found in the final sung notes of the opera, where in measure 1044 Nils sings the words *Fare thee well Oh! sweet silver stream* [173]: remembrances of the St. Johns river perhaps! The second *Irmelin* example, also an important theme, is found at measure 231 of Act II in the orchestral accompaniment [23]; the subject opens with a descending pentatonic passage which covers an octave in two measures and is clearly linked to themes from the *Cello Sonata* and the *Violin Sonata III* as can be seen in the comparative example 155.

A choral melody *Now once in a while,* which I believe to be of Afro-American origin, is found at the opening of Act II of *Koanga* [66]; it commences with an anacrusis before embarking on the transposed pattern *sol mi re*; the phrase occurs twice in the song. Another arch-shaped phrase appears in the closing five measures of *Koanga* played by the oboe and trumpet as a countermelody against the *Marching through Georgia* theme [94]. The *Cello Concerto* has two interesting subjects opening with this unit, namely the 6/4 solo cello melody appearing in measure 185 *molto tranquillo* [174 & composite ex. 202] and the impassioned violin I/violin II/flute call [175] found at *Rallentando* in measure 277 prior to the appearance of the closing subject. I feel that this concerto breathes the atmosphere of FD's earlier life in Florida without quoting any particular songs, simply by using note-patterns found in earlier works. Yet another example discussed above is the second subject or rather motive at measure 25 of the *Cello Sonata* [176]; it appears as a transposed version using *sol-mi-re* and the *sol* is approached by an anacrusis *la* a seventh lower. Later the *sol* is approached from above changing somewhat the character of the phrase, making the phrase peak on *la* instead of *sol,* and thereby changing the shape to a *la-sol-mi* post apex unit.

68   Group IX: 'Marching through Georgia' themes

Another group of melodies are those linked by Robert Threlfall in his article *Delius - Late Swallows in Florida* where he pointed to the similarity between the openings of themes from *Florida:* the flute melody commencing at cue 4 in the *Sunset* movement [177] from *Koanga,* the theme played by the cellos commencing at *andante tranquillo* eleven measures after cue 2 in the *Prologue* [178], and in the *String Quartet's Late Swallows* trio section melody, commencing at the double bar, six measures after cue 4 played by violin I [179].

They all start with what appears to be the opening phrase of the Civil War hymn *Marching through Georgia,* which I have combined with the *Koanga* theme in example 178 for comparison's sake. At first I assumed that the melody was derived from a spiritual, but in vain have I searched for an Afro-American melody that starts in this manner. The downward leap of the major sixth is often found in spirituals but never in an opening theme when the melody starts on the mediant. There is no point trying to squeeze a round peg into a square hole and since it also happens to be the opening of Henry C. Work's very well-known song, it is pointless assuming that the theme is of some other origin. Perhaps to FD this phrase represents 'The South', the Civil War and the resulting liberation of the slaves. One would expect him to use it in the two earlier pieces, but its use in the more abstract *String Quartet* suggests that perhaps FD had a personal program in mind when composing the work. Each of these melodies is typical of the composite melodic construction method used both by FD, as in the *Piano Concerto*, and, as originally suggested by Allen, Ware and Garrison [83 and later confirmed by Dorothy Scarborough, [84 by Black-Americans in religious and secular folk music from time to time.

PART FIVE / *Discussion of individual works*

69 Introduction to Part Five

It would seem logical to assume that the two images which are most frequently triggered off, the appearance of Afro-American melodies or techniques in FD's music are the concepts of 'Sunset' and 'The River', both of which stem from that 'moment of realisation' in Florida, and to a certain extent this is true.85 Take for example the *Sunset* movement from *Florida*, the second of the two songs *To be sung of a summer night on the water* and the close of the early song *Twilight Fancies*; however this is not always the case. For example, the early short orchestral piece *Summer Evening* [1890] contains no Afro-American influence that I can find whatsoever and in fact there is a marked indebtedness to a song by Grieg. The later work *Summer Night on the River* [1913] similarly seems to have no Afro-American influence. If there is a link between sections of works containing Floridian Afro-American influences it appears to be of an amatory nature or perhaps concerning an evening tryst which has already been hinted at when speaking of *Koanga* and which we will discover to be so later in sections devoted to *A Village Romeo and Juliet* and the *Songs of Sunset*.

As the reader will have noted, I have found that the number of FD's works using Afro-American techniques actually increased towards the end of his life to reach a climax in those pieces produced with the help of the young Eric Fenby. In the works of the middle period, the general Afro-American influence had become totally integrated and submerged into the general Delius style, but from 1914 onwards, Afro-American melodies and thematic fragments were used more and more frequently. The reasons for this are not hard to find. Delius's illness was becoming more and more serious resulting in complete paralysis and blindness by 1926; the 1914-18 war had naturally deprived him forever of the lion's share of his performances in Germany; and by 1922 he was entering his sixtieth year. Bearing this in mind, it is not at all surprising that nostalgia for an exciting and carefree period of his life should become so strong; to a blind man, the sound of the river Loing at the bottom of his garden would not have been difficult to transpose to a Floridian pitch. Several authorities have mentioned the nostalgia felt by FD near the end of his life for the American years. Eric Fenby describes it best when documenting the pleasure given to the composer by listening to a recording of the Revellers, quoted already in section 4: *Florida in retrospect* of this study.86

70 Florida [1887 rev. 1889]

It is the third movement, *Sunset*, in which I believe is found one of the few complete Afro-American melodies used by FD in his works; the others are the variation theme from *Appalachia* [6] and a melody in Act III of

Irmelin [62].* The *Florida* melody occurs in the *Danza* section [8] and is in 2/4; it is pentatonic except for a blue note which occurs in the second phrase; the note resolves in the normal way, and the repetition of the opening measures mark it as being of indisputably Afro-American origin.

The final movement *At Night* contains what appears to be an old hymn or spiritual which rather uncharacteristically is in triple time and, as with most of the Afro-American tunes Delius used, in the pentatonic scale [61]. FD varies the melody which is some eight measures in length. The form is a very simple *A B A B₁,* a form very important in the transition from the call and response form to that of a four line ballad used in spirituals and all later genre. The pitches used in *A* are a repeated *sol-la* while *B* utilizes *la do* and *re*. FD lengthens the melody and in so doing uses pitches foreign to the original pitch class.

Perhaps one of the most important technical developments which the young Fritz first used in the *Daybreak, By the River* and the *Sunset* movements of *Florida*, was the handling of background sixteenth-note continuum patterns already discussed in section 27: *Banjo (m'bira) and river-influenced accompaniments*; this concept was to be developed and used to such great effect in later masterworks such as the *String Quartet, Brigg Fair* and the *Violin Concerto*.

Mentioned in:

16 Afro-American influences - (The blues-slide used in the *Danza* section of *Sunset*)
26 Close relationship to the Dance - (The *La Calinda* and *Danza* sections of the *Daybreak* and *Sunset* movements)
27 'Banjo (m'bira)' and 'River' influenced accompaniments - (The *Danza* section of *Sunset*, and the oboe melody seven measures before cue 3 and seven measures before cue 5 of *Daybreak*)
28 Meter - (The *Danza* and *La Calinda* sections)
34 Descending (tumbling) tunes - (seven measures after cue 3 in *Daybreak*)
35 Pendulum and arch-shape melodies - (*La Calinda*)
36 Inverted arch-shaped melodies - (Fourteen measures after cue 4 in *Daybreak*)
37 Melodies using a limited note-set - (Measure 15 of *At Night*)
38 Blue-notes - (The *Danza* section of *Sunset*)
39 Repeated notes - (The *Danza* theme from *Sunset*)
40 Oscillating seconds and thirds - (The horn melody at measure 15 of *Night*)
41 Cadence patterns - (Internal cadences of the *Danza* and *La Calinda* sections)
43 The importance of *la* - (The oboe's melody in *Daybreak*, the *Danza* section of *Sunset*, and the spiritual-style melody in *At Night*)
44 The falling sixth: *sol-la-do* - (The *Marching through Georgia* composite theme at cue 4 of *Sunset*; found also in *Koanga* and *Late Swallows*)
45 A held note followed by multiple short notes - (The *Marching through Georgia* composite theme at cue 4 of *Sunset*; found also in *Koanga* and *Late Swallows*)
52 Delian turn IV: *sol-la-do la* - (The opening violin I/II pitches of the *Danza* section of *Sunset*)
57 Group I: *Possum up a gum-tree* and other songs - (The *Danza* section of *Sunset*)
58 Group II: Anacrusis/snap tunes - (The *Danza* melody from *Sunset*)
59 Group III: Cakewalk rhythm in the first measure of a theme - (The horn-call one measure before cue 2 of *Daybreak*)
68 Group IX: *Marching through Georgia* - (Cue 4 of *Sunset*)
69 Introduction to Part Five - (*Sunset* movement)

* [Thanks to an opportune discovery by Robert Threlfall in the Spring of 2001, a fourth complete Afro-American melody should be added here: the chorus *He will meet you when the sun goes down* from *Koanga*, already mentioned in this work's Preface.]

71 Twilight Fancies [1889-1890]

This early 'fairy-tale' song inhabits a Pre-Raphaelite world of princesses and horn calls which are evoked for the most part with Wagnerian stylings. At first sight the song appears to have few Afro-American characteristics until one comes to the cadence [3]. This mixing of European and Afro-American techniques is a characteristic of much of FD's music; however this does not seem to cause any lack of consistency to a modern listener, since our ability to spot these Afro-American fragments has long since been lost.

Mentioned in:
39 Repeated notes   -   (The cadence)
41 Cadence patterns   -   (The cadence)
65 Descending phrase using *la-sol-mi* after an apex   -   (*When the sun goes down*)
69 Introduction to Part Five   -   (The closing text)

72 Summer Evening [1890]

A work from the formative years, more Norwegian than American. Its main subject [109b] uses a a Grieg-inspired turn [109a].

Mentioned in:
39 Repeated notes   -   (The opening theme)
49 Delian-turn I: *mi-sol-la mi*   -   (The opening theme)
52 Delian-turn IV: *sol-la-do la*   -   (The opening triplet)
69 Introduction to Part Five   -   (General character)

73 Irmelin [1890-2]

There is much to find in this work that is germane to FD's development and also that which stems from his life in Florida; the influences are mainly in the details. The opera's first important motive occurs at the very start of the Prelude to Act I [52] and has much in common with other Delian and Afro-American themes as shown in composite music example 76. The particularly beautiful triplet decoration of the fall at measure 20 [158] is also worthy of comment. A *Possum up a Gum Tree* variant [135] has already been discussed in section 57. The melody commencing in measure 391 in Act III[62] is discussed in section 38: *Blue notes* together with two other examples. Furthermore, the importance of the *Appalachia*-style melody found at measure 135 of Act I [182 & 166] should be stressed.

The list of references made in this study to themes or motives found in *Irmelin* is considerable, but nonetheless I think that additional attention should also be drawn to the following. One of several short motives of possible Afro-American inspiration is found at measure 39 in the middle of the Prelude to Act III [183]. It is a balanced bow-shaped phrase using the complete ascending pentatonic pitches *do re mi sol la do*; on its descent it duplicates the first four pitches *do la sol re* at the lower octave thereby increasing the musical space occupied by the theme down another octave. It is related to the opera's opening statement, but the intervals have changed. Perhaps it is a variant or possibly a totally different theme; it appears frequently throughout the remainder of the score. This fragment acts as a prefix to the *Possum up a Gum Tree* influenced melody mentioned above.

Mentioned in:
29 The cakewalk rhythm   -   (Measure 231 of Act II)
34 Descending (tumbling) tunes   -   (Measure 231 of Act II)

35 Pendulum and arch-shaped melodies - (Opening orchestral motive)

38 Blue notes - (Measure 391 of Act III and measures 273 and 756 of Act II)

55 Sixteenth-note ornaments - (Measure 393 of Act III and birdsong.)

57 Group I: *Possum up a Gum Tree* and other songs - (Measure 43 in the Prelude to Act III)

61 Group Va: Ornamented slow cakewalk rhythm in the second measure preceded by a half note and two quarter notes - (Orchestral theme in measure 613 in Act II, also a motive found in Act I at measure 331 as well as the 3/2 theme at measure 231 of Act II)

63 Group Vc: Ornamented slow cakewalk rhythm in the second measure preceded by various rhythms - (Motive using triplet eighth notes in measure 20 of the opening of Act I)

64 Group VI: *Irmelin/Koanga/Appalachia* theme - (The Maid's melody measure 135 of Act I)

65 Group VIIa: Descending phrase using *la-sol-mi* after an apex - (Similarity of the orchestral theme at measure 231 of Act II to themes from the *Cello Sonata* and *Violin Sonata III*)

66 Group VIIb: Descending phrase using *do-te-sol* after an apex - (Opening theme)

67 Group VIII: Descending phrase using *do-la-sol* after an apex - (Measure 20 of Act I, measure 1044 of Act IV and measure 231 of Act II)

74 *Koanga [1895/7]*

Of all of FD's works, it is *Koanga* which has the most extended Black-American plot, and which would therefore give FD most reason to include Floridian and Virginian material. As time has passed it has become harder for us to recognise the 19th-century Black-Americaness of these tunes, since many of them tend to use the diatonic major scale. Attention has already been drawn to Sir Thomas Beecham's anecdote of the composer playing Afro-American melodies that he hoped to include in his forthcoming opera *Koanga* to friends (see section 5: *Florida in retrospect*).[87] It would be interesting to consider which were the melodies he incorporated into the opera if indeed he did use any of the pieces he played that day. We have already discovered that FD had a preference for secular over religious Afro-American melodies, many of which were diatonic, as opposed to the more easily recognizable pentatonic structures. The majority of secular melodies were never written down. Perhaps their appeal was less strong to later generations, and so unfortunately, a certain amount of subjectivity has to be involved. Notwithstanding there are three eight-measure melodies which have a marked Afro-American character and which have alredy been mentioned. They are:

1) the choral opening of Act II to the text *Now once in a way* [66]: 4/4, totally pentatonic, which makes much use of repeated-notes, and uses the transposed *do-la-sol* descending pattern. An interesting spiritual with the same rhythmic structure from the Civil War era is found in Barton's *Hymns of the Slave and the Freedman*, namely *O I'm goin' to sing*; these both appear together in example 189 for ease of comparison.

2) the Appalachian variant melody found in the chorus *He will meet her when the sun goes down* near the start of Act II [166]: 4/4, pentatonic except for a repeated eighth-note flattened *la* before the cadence, and making much use of repeated notes. This melody together with the variants found in *Irmelin* and *Appalachia* appear in a comparative grouping in exercise 166.

3) the soprano/tenor chorus part *Pa, he said son* of the tutti at cue 26 near the close of Act I [20]: 4/4 , much use of repeated notes, melody would be eight measures but for a doubling of the note lengths for the final line, uses cakewalk rhythm, lines two and three are pentatonic.

* [As mentioned in the *Preface*, Robert Threlfall of the Delius Trust published an article in the Autumn of 2001 regarding his discovery of a previously unknown manuscript containing several fragments of Afro-American origin. Included was an arrangement by FD of the above melody from *Koanga* entitled a *Negro Song* with a text commencing *I will meet you when the sun goes down.*]

Another similar pentatonic 4/4 theme of possible Floridian origin but somewhat longer first appears as a continuation of the *Marching through Georgia* theme eight measures before cue 3 in the Prologue. In Act II it is displayed as a melody in its own right directly after the opening chorus, and is played by the orchestra four times in succession; in each version the final cadence is varied, thereby giving the theme a somewhat open-ended feel.

The final version appears in the quodlibet-like section at cue 2 in the top voice [181]; the melody contains two measures of the cakewalk rhythm and many examples of the *Possum up a Gum Tree* melodic syncopation. This melody is grouped with other themes using the same climatic characteristics in the composite music example 202.

I have been unlucky in tracing any of the above secular-style melodies each of which I believe contains considerable Afro-American characteristics. This is hardly surprising since the amount of secular songs which have come down to us is so very sparse; but of course this could also mean that these songs are solely the work of FD in the Afro-American style.

Another shorter melody, four measures in length which seems to be derived in part from the *Appalachia* theme is that sung by Palmyra at cue 28 in Act I to the words *I feel a strange foreboding in my heart; this Voodoo Prince will bring me to my grave* [67]; it also is in 4/4, uses repeated notes, has a *me-do* cadence and has a transposed modally altered *do-la-sol* style climatic phrase in the third measure. With a certain sadness I have to state that by far and away the most famous section of *Koanga* is the *La Calinda* dance used also in *Florida*. It appears to contain no Afro-American characteristics whatsoever other than the repeated cakewalk rhythm accompaniment.

Mentioned in:

4   Florida in retrospect   -   (Sir Thomas Beecham's anecdote)
5   European influences   -   ('Old-plantation' feel)
28   Meter   -   (*La Calinda* dance in Act II and *John say you got to reap when you sow* chorus from Act I)
29   The cakewalk rhythm   -   (Chorus melody at cue 26 in Act I)
34   Descending (tumbling) tunes   -   (Six measures before cue 29 and ten measures after cue 5 in Act I)
35   Pendulum and arch-shaped melodies   -   (*La Calinda* dance and the tutti ensemble at cue 26 of Act I)
39   Repeated notes   -   (The chorus at the opening of Act II)
43   The importance of 'la'   -   (*Sol-la-do* pattern)
44   The falling sixth: *sol-la-do*:   -   (Rangwan's phrase thirteen measures after cue 9 in the final act, the
     Marching through Georgia theme from Act I, and Palmyra's phrase nine measures after cue 18 in Act III,
     and also the oboe phrase at the final cadence of the Epilogue)
45   A held note followed by multiple short notes   -   (*Marching through Georgia* theme found eleven measures
     after cue 2 in Act I)
50   Delian turn II; *la-sol-me la*   -   (Flute turn eight measures before cue 7)
52   Delian-turn IV: *sol-la-do la*   -   (Turn at *piu lento e tranquillo* seven measures after cue 13 in Act III)
53   Delian-turn V: *la-sol-mi sol*   -   (Cello turn in Act I commencing nine measures after cue 17, preceded by a
     chromatically altered version at cue 17)
54   Delian soaring triplet: *sol-la-do sol*   -   (Oboe triplet in Act I, six measures after cue 23)
64   Group VI: *Irmelin/Koanga/Appalachia* theme   -   (Chorus melody twelve measures before cue 3 in Act II)
67   Group VIII: Descending phrase using *do-la-sol* after an apex   -   (Oboe counter-melody in the closing five
     measures played against the *Marching through Georgia* theme, also the choral opening of Act II)
68   Group IX: *Marching through Georgia* themes   -   (First played eleven measures after cue 2 in Act I)
69   Introduction to Part Five   -   (*'Sunset', 'The River'* and *'Amatory'* concepts; see section 53)

75 *Romance for cello and piano [1896]*

A lyrical work from the early period similar in technique to that used in *Koanga* and *Florida,* it contains several characteristic units later used in more mature works; they include the soaring triplet figure, first used in measure five [123], an open-ended melody making important use of the *la* pitch found in the *molto tranquillo* sections together with groups of four ornamental sixteenth-notes used scalewise as in the *Song of Summer* and found in measures 67-69 at the end of the melody in the second *molto tranquillo* section [184].

Mentioned in:
54 Delian soaring triplet: s*ol-la-do sol* - (Variant form *mi-sol-re do* in measure 5)

76 *Piano Concerto [1897, rev. 1904, 1906-7 and 1909]*

This work which went through an unusually large number of metamorphoses certainly contained more than the normal amount of Afro-American music judging from reviews of Percy Grainger's performance with the NY Philharmonic in November, 1915. The program notes for the performance by W. H. Humiston contain an interesting statement about FD, namely that

*When he was about twenty he came to Florida to look after a plantation his father owned there, and he was so moved and stirred by the singing of the negro workers on the plantation that he decided to become a composer, and went to Leipzig to study.*88

Later on there is another perceptive quote:

'The theme of the slow movement (and in fact most of the themes) was composed in Florida and breathes American Southern feeling. The glowing warmth and wistful sentiment of this movement are indeed typical of Delius himself, yet they also recall the emotional quality of America's two enthralling composers - Stephen Foster and Edward MacDowell.

At no time does Humiston state that the themes were of Afro-American origin or inspired by Afro-American songs. In fact the critics were strongly divided as to how much Afro-American music appeared in the work and as to whether it was inspired by, or actually used, Afro-American melodies. Several critics mention the opening theme and the slow section melody as being inspired by an Afro-American song.89 The first movement's opening theme [38] is of the open-ended variety, the opening two measures of which certainly having all the necessary characteristics. It was not difficult finding Afro-American melodies beginning in this manner; the one with the strongest claim to be the inspiration for the theme is the riverboat song *Woman, Woman, I seen yo' man* [126] discussed numerous times above and which is combined with other Delian themes in example 126 for ease of comparison. Further insights into this historically important subject can be gathered from the composite examples 76 and 153.

Humiston's mention of Foster and MacDowell in his program note is particularly interesting. We know that FD had a passion for blackfaced minstrel music when young, so one assumes he must certainly have known Foster's most popular songs such as *Oh! Susanna, De Camptown Races* and *My Old Kentucky Home.* Indeed at this time it would have been hard not to have known these songs. MacDowell on the other hand is a different matter. Born two years earlier than FD, he also studied in Germany, Frankfurt & Wiesbaden, giving his first US public concert in 1888; he was active as a composer until 1904 living in Boston and later New York. It would seem unlikely that FD would have known much of his work other than the most popular pieces. That Humiston thought FD's *Piano Concerto* seemed similar to MacDowell's music is probably due to the influence of Grieg as well as each composer's interest in Afro-American music whether real or as heard through the filter of Foster and the minstrel composers.

The second principal theme in the first movement heard at *molto tranquillo*, three measures after cue 3 [82], is of a rather reflective nature and appears in marked contrast to the opening grand gestures. It is of an antiphonal type construction, in its first appearance alternating at two measure intervals between the horns, or brass, and the solo piano. If the ornamentation, a triplet followed by an eighth-note appoggiatura, is discounted, then we have in these three measures a common opening of slower spirituals. There are many examples to choose from, perhaps the best being one from John W. Work's collection, namely *Can't you live humble* [117] with its closing phrase using a retrograde *mi-sol-la* type FD triplet call; this turn is also much used in *Koanga* making numerous appearances between cue 17 and 18 in Act I [118].

In reality, there are only three themes of importance in the concerto. The third, the piano's *largo* section melody [58] is another question altogether. At first sight it appears to be the very soul of a slow spiritual, but after much searching I was unable to find any melody opening with a slow descending perfect fifth and then repeating the complete first measure three more times in the melody. In several cases melodies which jump a downward fifth insert an upper escape tone after the opening pitch thereby turning the perfect fifth into a major sixth. Melodies using a downward leap of a major sixth are far more common; the Afro-American obviously found the fifth not to his liking. It is not just the descending fifth that presents a problem but also the third note, a whole step above the B flat; these pitches *sol-do-re* simply do not normally appear in this style of music. This doesn't mean that the melody is not of Afro-American origin but rather that today we have no copy of it. Another work may give us the clue, the traditional spiritual *Nobody knows the Trouble I've seen* [90], which opens with *mi-sol-la-do* and then in measure three repeats the phrase; if the opening note *mi* is lowered a tone then we get the pitches of FD's opening measure. I feel that this is a composite melody made up of fragments of one or two other melodies as with the *Marching Through Georgia* themes found in *Late Swallows, Florida* and *Koanga* [177-179].

Mentioned in:
3   Leaves Florida for Virginia, New York and Leipzig - (Worked on *Piano Concerto* during second sojourn at Solano Grove)
8   River (rowing) songs - (Similarity of opening theme to *Woman, I seen yo' man*)
24   Call and response patterns - (Three measures after cue 3, and also at cue 6)
32   Anhemitonic pentatonic scale - (Opening theme)
34   Descending (tumbling) tunes - (Opening theme)
36   Inverted arch-shaped melodies - (Opening of the slow movement)
37   Melodies using a limited note-set - (Opening theme)
40   Oscillating seconds and thirds - (Piano at cue 3, and two measures before cue 24)
43   The importance of *la* - (Opening of the second subject three measures after cue 3)
52   Delian turn IV: *sol-la-do la* - (Opening pitches of the second subject)
53   Delian-turn V: *la-sol-mi sol* - (Opening of the second subject and the spiritual *Can't you live humble*)
54   Delian soaring triplet: *sol-la-do sol* - (Opening subject and the song *Woman, woman, I seen yo' man*)
57   Group I: *Possum up a Gum Tree* and other songs - (Subject II and the dance song *Hold my mule*)
61   Group Va: Ornamented slow cakewalk rhythm in the second measure preceded by a half note and two quarter notes - (Rhythmic structure of the piano's opening theme)
63   Group Vc: Ornamented slow cakewalk rhythm in the second measure preceded by various rhythms - (Simialarity of the rhythmic structure of the opening theme to the spiritual *Stand on a sea of glass*)
66   Group VIIb: Descending phrases using *do-te-sol* after an apex - (Opening theme)

77 Appalachia [1898-1903]

Delius's most popular work based on Afro-American music is the second version of *Appalachia*, subtitled *Variations on an old Slave Song with final chorus*. The melody used [6] is a rather simple one which he first heard sung in Florida and later in the Danville Stemmery Buildings and which I have been unable to trace in any song collection.90   It is built round a *C* major chord and first played by the cor anglais; the form of the variations is rather unique being basically what Grainger later termed 'passacaglia' type variations where the theme is sounded strictly throughout each variation against everchanging accompanying figures. But in this work, the variations are interspersed with contrasting sections based on new material.

The traditional variation form is of course the one beloved of the English Virginal School and Baroque composers in general. Delius was particularly drawn to this form, using it also in *Brigg Fair* and in a modified form in the first *Dance Rhapsody*. Arguably the most beautiful section, and most the characteristic of both FD and to the spirit of the Afro-American originators of the theme, is the final choral variation appearing some three quarters
of the way through the work at cue *Cc* utilizing a remarkably full chromatic harmonic palette. Shortly after this, a new melody appears to the words *O Honey, I am going down the river in the morning*; Clare Delius in her book *Frederick Delius: Memories of my Brother* attributed this second melody to Elbert Anderson, again it is major pentatonic and uses snap rhythms.

To a certain extent I believe that our perception of the choral sections of this work as being the typical 'Southern' Afro-American sound is partially due to the to the arrangements of spirituals by FD's contemporary Black composers, Henry T. Burleigh (1866-1949) [91] and J. Rosamond Johnson (1873-1954), [92] as much as to the improvised harmony of late 19th-century Afro-American singers of spirituals and secular songs. This has been discussed earlier in section 20: *The influence of Afro-American choral singing on the music of FD.*

Henry T. Burleigh is an important figure here. As a student of voice and composition he introduced spirituals to his teacher Dvorak at the National Conservatory in New York. I do not know if Burleigh knew the music of FD in his earlier years. Four years FD's junior, he arranged many of these in the early 1900s, using what was then fairly radical often chromatic chording; this style has stayed with this art form ever since. Whatever the origin for our accepting this as the typical 'Southern' sound, there is no denying the fact that FD has taken what must have been a very tentative chromaticism in the 1880s and lifting it to a far more exalted realm as in the final choral variation at cue *Cc* already mentioned.

Attention should also be drawn to the banjo-inspired stretto at *poco piu vivo ma moderato* [9] which leads into the first appearance of the variation theme, as well as to the cello's 6/8 *D* minor melody at cue J, *molto moderato,* [141] using dotted-notes, an anacrusis and a cadential snap at the close of the first phrase. The 6/8 time signature would seem to put this out of the realm of black music, but it should be remembered that several early songs use this time signature, and the melody does have many characteristics in common with songs such as the early 19th-century *Song of the Contrabands* [185]: the original ancestor of the spiritual *Go down, Moses.*93

Appalachia is an important pivotal work in that it bids farewell to Delius's formative years and heralds in a period which saw the creation of a large number of the composer's most representative works. It was a period of warm sonorities and of almost boundless inspiration. Of course to a subjective composer such as Delius, to whom each new work represented a fresh voyage, the question of inspiration was paramount. Note should also be made of the fact that during these years he entered the more austere Nordic world of Zarathustrianism. He was probably Nietzsche's most successful artistic convert, being true to this creed until death. Into this rarefied teutonic atmosphere, Florida and Afro-American culture had at best but a secondary place; however traces of the old love appeared from time to time. His mind had distilled many of the components of his Floridian experience, and these became part of his general creative palette.

Mentioned in:

78 A Village Romeo and Juliet [1900-01]

Like *A Mass of Life*, *A Village Romeo And Juliet* with its Northern setting and origin seems an unusual work in which to find much from his Florida days, but strangely enough it contains much that could be considered Afro-American in origin. For example, the opening melody [18] of *The Walk to the Paradise Garden*, and the blue notes in the oboe melody [64] have already been discussed. Also the opera's opening melody is of a pendulum nature and contains five appearances of the cakewalk rhythm within its ten measures [57]. One rather interesting fragment is found two measures after cue 17 in the second scene in which Vrenchen sings *I go t'wards evening out on the fields* [186]. The fragment has all the necessary characteristics: pentatonic scale, cakewalk rhythm, repeated notes and a common Afro-American cadence *la-do-re do* [119b]. It makes only one appearance but the cakewalk rhythm has been ushered in already.

Another important melody sung by Vrenchen appears at cue 6 at the start of Scene IV to the words *Ah, the night is approaching. Ah, the last night in my old home*; it is repeated six times in quick succession. The melody is in two phrases, one of two and the other of four measures; the scale is the Aeolian pentatonic mode commencing in *E flat* and finishing in *C minor*. After an initial leap upward of an octave from *G*, it falls slowly through the entire pitch series, closing on a low *E flat*; the pattern is then repeated but this time falling a twelfth and finishing with a *me-do* cadence in *C minor* rather similar to that found at the close of the *Appalachia* theme. The opening phrase of Vrenchen's song bears a marked similarity to a measure from the spiritual *I'm agoing to join the band* as shown in example 187.

An interesting shorter two-measure phrase worthy of comment is found in Scene VI; it is of a ritornello nature making a number of appearances and being sung to the words *Vagabonds are we* [88]. The phrase is tossed to and fro by a quintet in jocular fashion, and after making its first appearance at *comodo* one measure after cue 72, is repeated a number of times commencing six measures before cue 84. The first measure of the rhythm is a decorated cakewalk pattern and it uses three degrees from the pentatonic set - those venerable antique pitches *mi sol la*.

Another striking use of these pitches is found at the opening of Scene VI where the chorus sings using the pitches *sol mi la* to the text *Dance along, dance along further must we hie* [53]. It is from this motive that the *Vagabond* phrase is developed. Here we see the use of the 'shift' device; the first four measures are pentatonic, while the next phrase is heptatonic ending on a lower chromatic tone, the pattern being repeated for the final eight measures. The 6/8 time is no problem since in this case it is simply a rather flippant version of 2/4, the compound lilt giving it a dance-like character.

Mentioned in:
27 'Banjo (m'bira)' and 'River' influenced accompaniments - (Opening of Act I)
29 The cakewalk rhythm - (*The Walk to the Paradise Garden* and the opening theme of the opera)
32 Anhemitonic pentatonic scale - (Opening bassoon/horn melody from *The Walk to the Paradise Garden*).
35 Pendulum and arch-shaped melodies - (General)
36 Inverted arch-shaped melodies - (Opening of Act I)
37 Melodies using a limited note-set - (*The Walk to the Paradise Garden* opening bassoon/horn melody and one measure after cue 14)
38 Blue notes - (Oboe/cor anglais melody at cue 1 of *The Walk to the Paradise Garden*)
42 The 'shift' technique - (*Dance along* chorus at the start of Scene VI)
43 The importance of *la* - (Opening horn/bassoon melody from *The Walk to the Paradise Garden*, the chorus *Vagabonds are we* at cue 84 in the final scene, and the opening chorus of Scene VI *Dance along*)
54 Delian soaring triplet - *sol-la-do sol* - (*The Walk to the Paradise Garden* one measure after cue 2 and throughout the opera)
59 Group III: Cakewalk rhythm in the first measure of a theme - (Rhythmic structure of the opera's opening theme and the flute's melody at cue 15 of *The Walk to the Paradise Garden*)
60 Group IV: Ornamented cakewalk rhythm in the first measure of a theme - (Oboe's call three measures after cue 5 in Scene I)
62 Group Vb: Ornamented slow cakewalk rhythm in the second measure preceded by two eighth notes - (Cor anglais/bassoon/horn/viola motive three measures after cue 1)
65 Group VIIa: Descending phrase using *la-sol-mi* after an apex - (Vrenchen's repeated two measure phrase at cue 6 in Act IV)
69 Introduction to Part Five - ('Sunset', 'The River' and 'Amatory' concepts)

79 Sea Drift [1903/4]

Much to my surprise, I found little in this masterwork with its American setting to suggest that FD had ever lived in Florida. Granted the chorus's sublime entry *Once Paumanok, when the lilac scent was in the air* [2] with its low tessitura, falling chromatic lines, flattened (blue) sevenths, together with the important oboe turn which follows, have marked Floridian characteristics; but apart from these, the idiom seems mainly European with American nuance.

Mentioned in:
17 Prefered vocal tessituras - (Soprano part in alto range in the opening chorus *Once Paumanok*)
18 Vertical density - (Opening chorus *Once Paumanok*)
20 The influence of Afro-American choral singing on the music of FD - (Chorus's entry)
35 Pendulum and arch-shaped melodies - (General character)
46 A held note preceded by multiple short notes - (Oboe's turn at cue 3 after the chorus's entry)
51 Delian turn III: *sol-la-mi sol* or *sol-mi-la sol* - (Oboe's turn at cue 3 after the chorus's entry)
55 Sixteenth-note ornaments - (Horn's turn three measures before cue 22)

80 *A Mass of Life* *[1904-5]*

In a work with a text as inherently Germanic as that of *A Mass of Life*, one would expect to find little in the way of Afro-American melodies, and to a great extent that is so. However in the third movement, which opens with the words *In thine eye I gazed of late, O wondrous Life. Gold saw I in thy night-eye gleaming, My heart stood still - seized with voluptuous longing* [94, there are two important themes worthy of mention. The first is the alto's ritornello [97], a three-note rather sing-song phrase using the set *sol-la-do* very common in Delian turns. The 12/8 time-signature should not deter one from its origin; it merely gives it a rather relaxed 'swing' feel. The other theme is the *Possum up a Gum Tree* variant also sung by altos at the double bar at cue 19 [15].

Mentioned in:
27 'Banjo (m'bira)' and 'River' influenced accompaniments - (Chorus song at cue 19 in movement III)
35 Pendulum and arch-shaped melodies - (General character)
37 Melodies using a limited note-set - (Ritornello motive at start of movement III, also chorus song at cue 19)
39 Repeated notes - (Chorus song at cue 19 in movement III)
45 A held note followed by multiple short notes - (Ritornello motive at the start of movement III)
57 Group I: *Possum up a Gum Tree* and other songs - (Chorus song at cue 19 in movement III)

81 *Songs of Sunset* *[1906/7]*

A continuation of the stream of three extended masterworks for solo voices, chorus and orchestra commencing with *Sea Drift*. This work has more indebtedness to Afro-American music than do the other two, most of which is to be found in the form of orchestral motives. A transposed *mi-sol-la* three-note turn (*do-te-sol*) employs an inspired lower octave transfer on the third quarter-note, the motive makes its first appearance at the close of the first song played by the flute and cor anglais six measures after cue 4 [188]; the pitches are sounded nine measures earlier by the flute and clarinet using a different rhythm; the turn appears frequently in the other movements. A short melody using four pitches from the pentatonic set together with a repeated *sol-la-do* three-note turn is first played in octaves by the flute and oboe at the double bar at cue 15 in the third song [189]; a variant of this phrase using the full pentatonic set is later played by the clarinet three measures after cue 16. The developed theme, which now has a tumbling character, is played by the horns six measures later.

A singularly fine four-measure Dorian melody is played by the cor anglais in the fifth song at *slower* eight measures after cue 29 [39]; it makes frequent appearances thereafter. The older 'Southern' country blues and work songs frequently utilize the pitches *do-me* for the first section of the song, while the second half uses the minor third *la-do*; sometimes passing-tones are inserted and occasionally a short neighbor-note will appear extending the range down to *sol*. Such a Dorian melody is this; the heavy humid atmosphere is unmistakable.

The text speaks of *the sound, of waters of separation surpasseth roses and melody*. The choral close of the sixth song four measures before cue 41 [73] has already been discussed in sections 38: *Blue notes* and 40: *Oscillating seconds and thirds*. The hard-to-bear beauty and sadness is so very intense. Suffice to recall the text *But the flowers of the soul, for you and for me bloom never again*. Even the close of the final song uses an ornamented version of the Afro-American *la-do* cadence. The melody over the final chord however makes use of an appoggiatura *re* resulting in a *9-8* sounded-suspension, whilst clarinet I plays the *mi-sol-la* turn mentioned above [190].

Mentioned in:
17 Preferred vocal tessituras - (Chorus four measures before cue 41)
33 Mixolydian and other modes - (Cor anglais solo in the sixth song at *slower*, three measures before cue 30, also played by the first violins, four measures after cue 41)

38   Blue notes - (Chorus four measures before cue 41)

40   Oscillating seconds and thirds - (Chorus four measures before cue 41)

55   Sixteenth-note ornaments - (Flute/cor anglais's motive six measures after cue 4, also found in *Irmelin* and *Cynara*)

61   Group Va: Ornamented slow cakewalk rhythm in the second measure preceded by a half note and two quarter notes - (Rhythmic structure of the cor anglais's Dorian motive three measures before cue 30)

69   Introduction to Part Five - (Text of an amatory nature)

82   Brigg Fair [1907]

As the subject matter would denote, very little specific Afro-American influence is to be found here other than that found in the general Delian compositional style such as the <u>me-do</u> final cadence of the Lincolnshire folk song.

Mentioned in:

4   Florida in retrospect - (Radio broadcast conducted by Sir Thomas Beecham)

26   Close relationship to the dance - (Variations from cue 7 to 15)

27   'Banjo (m'bira)' and 'River' influenced accompaniments - (Violin I running sixteenth note counter-melody, *very lightly* at cue 9)

35   Pendulum and arch-shaped melodies] - (General character)

41   Cadence patterns - (Cadence of the theme)

45   A held note followed by multiple short notes - (Flute arabesques at the opening, also at cues 15 and 28)

55   Sixteenth-note ornaments - (Flute arabesques at the opening, also clarinet I in the fourth measure)

83   In a Summer Garden [1908 rev.1911]

Like *Paris* and *Brigg Fair*, this is a very European work having little if anything from the Florida years about it. In his preface to the score FD mentions *roses, lilies,* and *flows a quiet river water-lilies* and also *a thrush singing - in the distance,* [95 obviously the Loing and not the St. Johns river; furthermore the work was a present to Jelka. Worthy of note are the flowing woodwind eighth notes in the center section representing the flowing river at the slow center section of the work six measures before cue 11 [191] and what I thought could possibly be a blue note in an oboe phrase six measures after cue 24, but a closer inspection of the underlying harmony makes its provenance European. A case could perhaps be made for considering the staccato sixteenth-note 'bird songs' found so frequently throughout the work to be of American origin because of the *Possum up a Gum Tree* pattern used, but again I feel that this was possibly not FD's intention [136].

Mentioned in:

27   'Banjo (m'bira)' and 'River' influenced accompaniments - (Flute and oboe's legato broken-chord patterns)

57   Group I: *Possum up a Gum Tree* and other songs - (Oboe's tumbling sixteenth-note phrase in measure six)

84   A Dance Rhapsody I [1908]

A Northern work with the odd touches of Afro-Americaness about it such as the cadence of the oboe's main theme [74 & 119a]. This dotted-note theme is almost certainly not inspired by Afro-American vocal music, although a banjo or violin provenance is possible.

Mentioned in:

5   European influences - (Grainger's comments regarding the cadence of the oboe's subject at cue 2)
19 Husky or raucous tone - (Use of the bass oboe)
26 Close relationship to the dance - (General character)
28 Meter - (2/4 meter)
30 Triplets and dotted notes - (Main oboe subject at cue 2)
33 Mixolydian and other modes - (Main oboe subject at cue 2)
41 Cadence patterns - (Afro-American cadence of the main oboe subject at cue 2)

85 Midsummer Song [1908]

A delightfully flippant miniature, perhaps reminiscent of the idealized dreamworld of the American painter Maxfield Parrish.

Mentioned in:
18 Vertical density - (Use of eight parts)
26 Close relationship to the dance - (General dance-like character)
27 'Banjo (m'bira)' and 'River' influenced accompaniments - ('Plucked' accompaniment)
28 Meter - (6/8 time signature)

86 The Song of the High Hills [1911]

This is another of FD's works with a definite Nordic slant, but it contains an important theme which I believe to be of Floridian inspiration or origin. It is the eight-measure melody, a rarity in the composer's output, which first appears at the *very slow* section commencing six measures before cue 18 and played in octaves by divided first violins and then by the first oboe [157]. It is later sung by the wordless chorus at *slow and very legato* at cue 30. This is another of one of the composer's 'moments of realization' choruses, complete with chromatically descending accompanying voices, which appear at points of great serenity in the composer's output.

The theme fits easily into two-bar units although FD phrases it in 2+2+4 sections. The melody is in the natural minor with the first phrase having a falling *re-te sol* phrase at the start of the second measure which uses the ornamented cakewalk rhythm discussed in sections 60-63. This rhythmic structure gives it similarities with themes from *Irmelin* and the *Piano Concerto* which are displayed together in musical example 153. The second phrase has the repeated quarter notes on beats two and three found in the *Possum up a Gum Tree* song discussed in section 57. The third two-measure phrase is of a tumbling pentatonic nature covering an octave in five beats whilst the closing two measures use a minor version of the *mi-re-do* cadence found at the identical place in the well-known children's song *Short'nin' Bread* [87]. This cadence is also found in the popular dance song *Jump Jim Crow* [192] which appears in Dorothy Scarborough's collection; this immensely popular song was adapted by the famed Minstrel Show musician 'Jim Crow' Rice, as he was later to be called, from a traditional 'Negro' folk-song he first heard in Louisville, Kentucky.96 An alternative and equally well known origin for this cadential phrase is to be found at the close of Stephen Foster's well-loved minstrel song *Old black Joe*.

In short, FD's melody is not in the very common pentatonic major but in the somewhat rarer natural minor also preferred by Afro-Americans. Each of the four two-measure phrases has Black characteristics although I sense that the whole has a somewhat 'assembled' feel, as indeed also does the theme from the slow section of the *Piano Concerto* [58] or the *Marching through Georgia* melodies [177-179]. This is not surprising since as Allen, Ware and Garrison have pointed out, 19th-century Afro-Americans were also disposed to use this method of composition.97

Mentioned in:

18 Vertical density - (Eight-part choral section at cue 30)

20 The influence of Afro-American choral singing on the music of FD - (Chromatic writing in the eight-part choral section at cue 30)

35 Pendulum and arch-shaped melodies - (General character)

45 A held note, followed by multiple short notes - (Oboe phrase at *In tempo* four measures after cue 23)

51 Delian turn III: *sol-la-mi sol* or *sol-mi-la sol* - (Chromatic version one measure after cue 3)

57 Group I: *Possum up a Gum Tree* and other songs - (Minor variant of this song one measure before cue 31)

62 Group Vb: Ornamented slow cakewalk rhythm in the second measure, preceded by two eighth notes - (Chorale-like theme at *very slow* seven measures after cue 17)

63 Group Vc: Ornamented slow cakewalk rhythm in the second measure preceded by various rhythms - (Similarity of the chorale-like theme seven measures after cue 17 to the spiritual *Stand on a sea of glass*)

66 Group VIIb: Descending phrase using *do-te-sol* after an apex - (Phrase shape of the fifth measure of the chorale-like theme)

87 *On hearing the first cuckoo in spring [1912]*

This beautiful and much-loved miniature is a typical creation of FD's middle years and is based on the Norwegian folksong *In Ola Dal*. Other than the general Afro-American characteristics that shaped the Delian style, there is little else to be found here as would be expected,

Mentioned in:

35 Pendulum and arch-shaped melodies - (General character)

50 Delian turn II: *la-sol-me la* - (Oboe turn in measure two)

88 *I-Brasil [1913] and other songs*

FD's songs have singularly little of the Floridian years about them with the exception of *I-Brasil*, a miniature masterwork which blends the idioms of the Hebrides with that of the New World to the west mainly through the handling of dotted notes and snaps [27]. Another favorite song, *Black Roses* (1901), has what could possibly be regarded as a blues third in the final phrase to the text of *for sorrow has night-black roses!* [193]. The early song *The Homeward Way* (1889) is mainly in the traditional idiom of the day. Like *Twilight Fancies* it contains points of interest in the closing measures, namely a soaring triplet [194] in the piano six measures before the close, a blues seventh in the final vocal phrase [195], and in the final two measures, the previous piano triplet evolves into what appears be an early version of a triplet turn [196].

Mentioned in:

30 Triplets and dotted notes - (*I-Brasil* - General rhythmic character)

41 Cadence patterns - (*I-Brasil* - Piano introduction)

89 *Summer Night on the River [1911]*

I can find no Afro-American influence here despite the title. The descending jump of the <u>minor</u> sixth in the main 6/4 theme is definitely not an Afro-American characteristic; see section 44: *Sol-la do: the falling sixth.*

Mentioned in:

69 Introduction to Part Five - (No 'Sunset' or 'River' influence)

90 North Country Sketches [1913/14]

A fine work with many strokes of the master orchestrator's genius but none too popular with Delius aficionados, probably because of its somewhat dissonant harmonic palette; for example quartal harmony is used in the opening movement. FD introduces many themes possibly inspired by the folk song and dance of the North of England which often shares characteristics with Gaelic and Afro-American music. For example the very strong opening snap found in the tutti march-like tune which makes its appearance three measures after cue 53 in *The March of Spring* [197] is, I feel, Gaelic or Northern English in its inspiration. Contrast this with a similar strings and brass melody at cue 25 of *Dance* [198] in which the use of the snap/ dotted-note unit is gentler, and so a possible Floridian origin is suggested. This opinion is reinforced when one considers the *la-do-re-do* cadence [119a]. This all of course almost borders on the subjective, but the melodies' origin could be as a possible outgrowth of earlier Afro-American melodies such as the 6/8 cello theme at cue J from *Appalachia* [141].

Another point of interest is the main legato theme of *Winter Landscape* which metamorphosed out of the cello melody at cue 11 of the opening *The Wind soughs in the trees* . This melody changes its mode depending on its accompaniment, for example Mixolydian at cue 16. Its final appearance in *F* [199] contains an opening flattened seventh (*E flat*), a sharpened fourth (*B natural*) leading to a minor third (*A flat*), each of which is a characteristic pitch of the blues scale. All of this over a *D flat/A flat* pedal!

Mentioned in:
41 Cadence patterns - (Afro-American cadence patterns found in the *Dance* movement)
51 Delian turn III: *sol-la-mi sol* or *sol-mi-la sol* - (Flute/oboe's turn one measure before cue 5)

91 Requiem [1914/16]

This is a very controversial work, controversial because of its text rather than its music. It contains a very important section between cues 23 and 28 which metamorphoses a Delian turn from a four-note descending chromatic scale into a turn using the pitches *sol-la-do la* [200]. The text speaks of love, *My beloved whom I cherished* and at two- or three-measure intervals a turn is sounded, always slightly varied and mostly played by solo woodwind instruments against a string and choral continuum. This general concept puts it in line with many symphonic development sections from Mozart and Beethoven, but of course the aural effect is quite different. Both the text and the use of the turn, if not inspired by FD's period in Florida, is at least totally compatible with musical concepts from that period of his life.

Mentioned in;
24 Call and response patterns - (Opening measure)
25 Improvisation (variation) - (Turns throughout Movement III)
52 Delian-turn IV: *sol-la-do la* - (Turns throughout Movement III)
60 Group IV: Ornamented cakewalk rhythm in the first measure of a theme - (Oboe/cor anglais's phrase one measure before cue 25 in Movement III)

92 Violin Sonata I [1905 & 1914]

This of all the late sonatas possesses the least amount of Afro-American influence, seemingly inhabiting the more refined world of contemporary French music. The slow section nevertheless uses a two-measure motive utilizing an ornamentation of the cakewalk rhythm [203], making almost continual use of the pendulum shape and also the descending sixteenth-note ornamental pattern already mentioned in section 55. This motive is compared to themes from spirituals and other works in example 208.

Mentioned in:

46 A held note preceded by multiple short notes - (Violin's turns at *piu tranquillo e piu lento*)

55 Sixteenth-note ornaments - (Violin's theme of the *slow* section)

93 *Air and Dance* [1915]

In her book *The Road to Samarkand,* Gloria Jahoda writes on page 180 that *Philip [Heseltine] had rekindled Florida memories. An Air and Dance Delius composed was full of tiny snatches of Negro blues.*98 This short very easygoing work contains much of interest including a very kaleidoscopic approach to tonality. The opening melody commences with *do-re do-ti la-sol la-ti do* in G major [28] which FD harmonizes in a short-lived *C* major tonal center but with many unresolved secondary dominant sevenths. The early emphasis on *la* straight away gives a Floridian feel to the work, but as the movement progresses, the opening *do* frequently becomes the third of the chord thereby turning the pitch *la* into *do*. Frequently the modality of the motive is changed by chromatically lowering the *re* pitch. There appears to be only one example of a blue note in the main soprano voice; it occurs fifteen measures into the *Dance* section where a *D sharp* resolves onto an *E natural* [201]. I can see how easy it is to mistake the presence of the blue notes from an aural point of view, since the middle and lower voices are in an almost perpetual chromatic state, resulting in a very vague sense of tonality despite the fact that chromatics are rare in the top voice. Very often one gets the impression that the chromatic harmony represents the tonal center while the diatonic melody note appears to be a chromatic blue note.

Mentioned in:

30 Triplets and dotted notes - (The dotted notes in both movements)

94 *Double Concerto* [1915/16]

Each of the three concerti written during this late period have whole internal sections devoted to Afro-American inspired melodies. The first of these, the *Double Concerto* for violin and cello written in 1915 is thought to be autobiographical. Delius was deeply affected by the war and the work contains much of a funereal, as well as a mystical nature. As with his other concerti, this work is in one movement but nevertheless falls generally into the traditional three sections. The first reaches its climax at cue 17 before quickly subsiding into the section marked *Slowly and Quietly* where an old Florida Hymn *Sing to Mary* (pentatonic and in 4/4 time) 99 is introduced by the horns and cor anglais before being finally stated by the solo cello [59]; this theme is used throughout the entire section.

Mentioned in:

35 Pendulum and arch-shaped melodies - (*Sing to Mary* solo cello melody at *slow,* cue 18)

42 The 'shift' technique - (*Sing to Mary* solo cello melody at *slow,* cue 18)

95 *A Dance Rhapsody No. 2* [1916]

Since most of this rhapsody is in triple time, it would seem that the quotation of any Afro-American melodic fragments would be unlikely, but there are three points worthy of mention. The first is the rising third cadence *do-me* (or *la-do)* in the flute's opening melody in measure 4 [159]; the second is the oboe's melody at measure 147 [160] with its rhythmic pattern derived from an adaption of the cakewalk rhythm discussed in section 63; and the last is the sarabande rhythm used in alternate measures in the tutti section at cue 220 already discussed in section 29.

Mentioned in:
29 The cakewalk rhythm - (3/4 adaption of a 4/4 rhythmic pattern in measure 220)
55 Sixteenth-note ornaments - (Flute's angular motive at measure 266)
63 Group Vc: Ornamented slow cakewalk rhythm in the second measure, preceded by various rhythms -
   (3/4 adaption of a 4/4 rhythmic pattern in measure 147)

96 Violin Concerto [1916]

Delius's next concerto, and probably his most successful, was the *Violin Concerto*. Its sections are far more varied than those in the other concerti, but still the overall design is basically Moderato - Adagio - Allegretto. The central slow section alternates between a first theme having what could best be described as a languorous arabesque quality, this being followed by a falling pentatonic theme using a snap rhythm on the first beat of every measure [35]. This melody with its opening phrase being a transposed version of the pitches *mi-sol-la* is of course a very ancient pattern found in music of many cultures. In fact the opening two measures of this theme are remarkably similar to those found in the first subject of the *Piano Concerto* [38] but with a different rhythmic structure. The *Violin Concerto* theme may of course be totally FD's work and not an Afro-American melody. If this is the case then it proves the power that the steamboat song *Woman, woman, I seen yo' Man* still held in FD's musical memory; this similarity can be clearly seen in the grouping of themes in example 126.

It is important to point out at this juncture that one of Delius's favorite gramophone records was of Hebridean folk songs,[100] and much of Hebridean folk music uses both the pentatonic scale and snap rhythms. It could be difficult to tell the inspiration for such a melody, since if you transpose it up some two octaves, rob it of any characteristic Afro-American or Scottish performance practices and introduce into it all the elegant nuances added by an art music performer, then much of the original nature of the theme is lost. Subjectively speaking, I feel that because of the way the melody uses the snap rhythms, together with its irregular 'gapped' pentatonic descending sequential shape and the tumbling nature in general, then the melody is almost certainly of Afro-American or even African origin. As I listen to the various statements of this theme, I become more sure as to its origin; I feel the warmth of Florida prevails.

Mentioned in:
26 Close Relationship to the dance - (12/8 final section)
27 'Banjo (m'bira)' and 'River' influenced accompaniments - (Solo violin's sixteenth note counter melody at
   cue 32)
31 The Afro-American snap-rhythm - (Violin I's *D* minor theme at cue 19 in the slow section)
32 Anhemitonic pentatonic scale - (Violin I's *D* minor theme at cue 19)
34 Descending (tumbling) tunes - (Violin I's *D* minor theme at cue 19, also the first movement's opening
   solo violin theme)
35 Pendulum and arch-shaped melodies - (General characteristics)
38 Blue notes - (Solo violin's phrase at cue 15)
39 Repeated notes - (Violin I's *D* minor theme at cue 19)
40 Oscillating seconds and thirds - (Violin I's *D* minor theme at cue 19)
41 Cadence patterns - (Afro-American phrase endings found in the slow section)
42 The 'shift' technique - (Solo violin's 'combination' melody at cue 14 in the slow section)
54 Delian soaring triplet: *sol-la-do sol* - (Similarity of slow section's subject to the opening theme of the
   Piano Concerto)
55 Sixteenth-note ornaments - (Solo violin's opening subject)
59 Group III: Cakewalk rhythm in the first measure of a theme - (Rhythmic structure of the opening
   measures)

61   Group Va: Ornamented slow cakewalk rhythm in the second measure preceded by a half note and two quarter notes - (Rhythmic structure of the solo violin's opening statement)

63   Group Vc: Ornamented slow cakewalk rhythm in the second measure preceded by various rhythms - (Similarity of the slow movement theme to the opening theme of the *Piano Concerto*)

97   Cello Sonata   [1916]

The second of the solo sonatas, like all of FD's works for solo cello, appears to contain much influence from his youthful orange farming years. A very cyclic work, almost monothematic. The first movement opens in *D* major, or possibly the natural version of *B* minor, with both instruments having important motives. The piano's phrase [204] is transformed into the first movement's second subject [205] which is further metamorphosed into the slow movement's main theme and possibly derived from a spiritual in the natural minor [155]; the final movement is a varied recapitulation of the opening movement. Of further interest is the marked similarity of the slow section's theme at *lento, molto tranquillo* in measure 127 to a phrase in the Prelude to Act I of *Irmelin* at measure 20 [158] and to the important two-measure theme found at measure 231 in Act II [23]. Each one of these subjects is combined in the three comparative musical examples, numbers 67, 155 and 205 for the sake of clarity.

Mentioned in:

29   The cakewalk rhythm - (Similarity of theme at measue 127 to themes from *Irmelin* and *Violin Sonata III*)

61   Group Va: Ornamented slow cakewalk rhythm in the second measure, preceded by a half note and two quarter notes - (Cello's melody at measure 127 at *lento, molto tranquillo*)

62   Group Vb: Ornamented slow cakewalk rhythm in the second measure, preceded by two eighth notes - (Subject at measures 25 and 44 of the opening movement)

65   Group VIIa: Descending phrase using *la-sol-mi* after an apex - (Similarity of the theme at measure 127 to subjects from *Irmelin* and *Violin Sonata III*)

67   Group VIII: Descending phrases using *do-la-sol* after an apex - (Subject at measures 25 and 44 of the opening movement)

98   String Quartet   [1916/17]

At first sight it would seem that a supposedly abstract work like a *String Quartet* is an unlikely place to look for Afro-American influences partly because of the use of triple and compound time in the first two movements; both times being rare in spirituals and work songs but at the same time very common in African music. Percy Grainger has noted that FD favored the use of Afro-American cadence patterns in his melodies.[101]

In this work, FD makes use of an appoggiatura on the final note of a cadence, this ornament is very common particularly in spirituals. The grace note is frequently fairly short, although slow appoggiaturas are found. Percy Grainger noted that FD favored the use of cadence patterns used in spirituals and secular songs; this work is of no exception. A particularly fine example is found in the final cadence of the first movement [49]: violin I moves from a high *do*, down to a blue *fi*, which resolves into *sol*, then to *te* and finally to the appoggiatura *me-do*, the violin being doubled two octaves lower by the cello making a very strong and striking effect! The opening motive of the second movement also uses an appoggiatura at the phrase's close [206] which seems derived from the previous movement's final cadence; this time we have *do le-fa-sol me-do* compared to the previous *do fi-sol-te me-do*; the pattern also appears at two-measure intervals in the movement's final 13 measure coda.

The same minor third pattern appears numerous times in the section commencing at measure 9 in the final movement before becoming part of the cello's main subject in measures 5 & 6 [83]. The descending minor third appears 18 times in the first violin part of the final codetta. In fact I feel that the opening of this subject is a distant descendent of the banjo *Danza* from *Florida* [8] and has a number of characteristics similar to FD's earlier composite tunes containing a number of past remembered fragments of melodies. This observation brings us to the *Late Swallows* movement; the final two-measure phrase of the *Marching through Georgia* trio melody [119b] seems very familiar and yet is elusive; this cadential pattern is common in spirituals and is also found in a variant from *A Village Romeo and Juliet*, but I've been unable to locate it with this particular rhythmic structure.

Mentioned in:
27 Banjo (m'bira) and river-influenced accompaniments - (Four measures after cue 3 of *Late Swallows*)
34 Descending (tumbling) tunes - (Closing phrase of the first movement)
38 Blue notes - (Closing phrase of the first movement)
40 Oscillating seconds and thirds - (Violin I bridge-section at cue 8 of *Late Swallows*, also in measure 10 of the final movement)
41 Cadence patterns - (Closing phrase of the first movement, also three measures before cue 8 of *Late Swallows*, and at measure ten in the final movement)
44 The falling sixth: *sol-la-do*: - (*Marching through Georgia* theme six measures after cue 4 in *Late Swallows*, also one measure after cue 21 in the final movement)
45 A held note followed by multiple short notes - (*Marching through Georgia* theme in *Late Swallows*)
53 Delian-turn V: *la-sol-mi sol* - (Close of *Marching through Georgia* melody two measures after cue 5 in *Late Swallows*)
57 Group I: *Possum up a Gum Tree* and other songs - (Cello theme from movement IV at *with bright and elastic movement*, four measures before cue 3)
66 Group VIIb: Descending phrase using *do-te-sol* after an apex - (Reappearance of Afro-American stylings in later works)
68 Group IX: *Marching through Georgia* themes - (*Late Swallows* movement six measures after cue 4)

99 To be sung of a summer night on the water [1917]

These two unaccompanied part-songs are in my opinion one of the finest works from FD's middle period. This beautiful diptych captures perfectly the character of the two rivers, the Loire and the St Johns; the first has the character of a slow gavotte and therefore an antique European feel, although the harmonies may have a Floridian origin. The second song uses a melody of the *Possum up a Gum Tree* type already discussed in sections 35, 55 and 57. The short pentatonic theme [54] is repeated seven times and sung for the most part by a solo male voice: echoes of Elbert Anderson. The melody has all the characteristics of the banjo melody from the thirf movement of *Florida* as well as those of the fiddle tune *Roaring River* [207] notated in 1853. As one would expect, the opening phrases of these melodies fills the pitches of the pentatonic collection upwards from *sol* to *mi*, the interval of a major sixth.

Mentioned in:
26 Close relationship to the dance - (Gavotte nature of first song)
35 Pendulum and arch-shaped melodies - (Second song)
39 Repeated notes - (Second song)
55 Sixteenth-note ornaments - (Ornament in first measure of second song)
57 Group I: *Possum up a gum-tree* and other songs - (Solo tenor melody of second song)
69 Introduction to Part Five - (Second song regarding 'Sunset' and 'The River')

100 A Song before Sunrise [1918]

Very often when composing works of a nocturnal character, FD would make use of material from the American years, but not this time. This miniature, dedicated to Philip Heseltine was inspired by a chapter from *Thus spake Zarathustra.*

Mentioned in:
28 Meter - (6/8 time signature)

101 Intermezzo and Serenade from Hassan [1920/23]

The *Serenade* is one of FD's most popular creations, and rightly so, containing a few Delian characteristics of possible American ancestry. The main point that I find interesting is found in the melody [93] at measure 3, already discussed in section 44: *Sol-la do: the falling sixth.* The strong beat *la* is preceded and followed by *sol* which serves to highlight the pitch and to link it to other themes as shown in composite example 84. This phrase appears a total of seven times in the *Serenade's* thirty-seven measures. Of interest also is the melodic cadence *do-re-mi* found in the second half of the same measure and which occurs eight times in *F* and once in *C*. This cadence is identical to that found in the song *Jordan Mills* [16] from Virginia quoted in *Slave Songs of the United States* and already discussed in sections 28 and 41 thereby giving further credence to the possibility that FD knew and admired this spiritual. The cadences from the *Serenade* and *Jordan Mills* are combined together in exercise 93 for ease of comparison.

The *Intermezzo* contains far more material showing American influence. For example the motives are frequently pentatonic using typical sixteenth-note ornaments as well as an ornamented cakewalk rhythm and a Delian triplet turn (*sol-do-la sol*) in measures six, seven, eight and ten. The motive stated by the clarinet in measure five is displayed with other themes in the composite example 208.

Mentioned in:
28 Meter - (Relaxed 6/4 meter)
41 Cadence patterns - (Similarity of the cadence from *Serenade* to that found in the spiritual *Jordan's Mills*)
44 The falling sixth: *sol-la-do* - (Filled-in downward leap)
46 A held note preceded by multiple short notes - (The opening cello theme from the *Intermezzo*)
55 Sixteenth-note ornaments - (The opening cello theme from the *Intermezzo*)
60 Group IV: Ornamented cakewalk rhythm in the first measure of a theme - (The opening cello theme from the *Intermezzo*)

102 Cello Concerto [1921]

The last of the three concerti abounds with melodic fragments conjuring up the mood Stephen Foster sought to recapture; sunny pentatonic melodies often with a rather easy laid-back rhythmic feel prevail throughout. Since almost all of the concerto is in triple or at least compound time, and as mentioned before regarding the *String Quartet*, this makes the inclusion of Afro-American melodies unlikely. Bearing this in mind, I believe that FD used many melodic units as well as cadence patterns which I feel originated from the Florida years. Most of the characteristic themes have already been mentioned, they include:

i)   the 6/4 string theme at *lento* measure 93 [81], the opening measures of which use the pentatonic scale, and later the 'shift' technique,

ii) the turn at measure 277 [175] using the *do-la-sol* note-set, and

iii) the 12/8 theme played by the first violins at measure 36 [85] using an opening blue note at its commencement, which is omitted from the cello's version played six measures later, making the phrase totally pentatonic. This and two other themes from the concerto sharing characteristics in common, are grouped together in composite example 202.

Another theme worth drawing attention to is the solo cello's legato melody at cue 290 [22] in the work's closing section. The melody begins with a very marked sixteenth-note 'tumble' down an octave in a mere three and a half beats before slowly moving upward via an appoggiatura *A* to *B* and then continuing its ascent up to *G* using only the pitches of the pentatonic scale with the exception of a sixteenth-note *F sharp*. The appoggiatura in measure 292 is very characteristic of 19th-century Afro-American song while the elongated second beat gives a cakewalk feel to many measures even though the time is 3/4. This important subject is shown with other similar themes in the composite example 208. If one thing is needed to be emphasized pointing to the Afro-American feel to much of the concerto, I feel that it is the relative importance given melodically to the *la* scale degree.

Mentioned in:
28 Meter - (General character)
29 The cakewalk rhythm - (Solo cello theme at measure 290 *piu lento, molto tranquillo*)
38 Blue notes - (Opening of violin I's two measure melody at measures 36 and 38)
42 The 'shift' technique - (The 6/4 pentatonic string theme at measure 93 *lento*)
43 The importance of *la* - (First violin and cello hemiola motive in measure 158 *poco piu mosso*)
46 A held note preceded by multiple short notes - (Solo cello theme at measure 290 *piu lento, molto tranquillo*, also its development at measure 310)
52 Delian-turn IV: *sol-la-do la* - (Solo cello theme at measure 41; not a turn, but uses the turn pitches)
55 Sixteenth-note ornaments - (Solo cello melody at measure 290 *piu lento, molto tranquillo*)
60 Group IV: Ornamented cakewalk rhythm in the first measure of a theme - (Rhythmic structure of the cello's final theme at measure 290)
66 Group VIIb: Descending phrase using *do-te-sol* after an apex - (Reappearance of Afro-American stylings in later works)
67 Group VIII: Descending phrase using *do-la-sol* after an apex - (Flute/violin I and II descending turn-like motive at measure 277 *rallentando*)

103 Violin Sonata II [1923]

Another inspired masterwork from FD's mature years showing his total command and understanding of the use of *melos*. This work has more than its share of blue notes, and the jaunty, tumbling dotted note unit first found in the *poco meno mosso, piu tranquillo* section [209] could have Floridian ancestry; this phrase is preceded by a repeated Delian turn [169] of the *la-sol-mi* variety discussed in section 53.

Mentioned in:
46 A held note preceded by multiple short notes - (Violin's four measure melody at *piu tranquillo e piu lento* before *lento*)
65 Group VIIa: Descending phrases using *la-sol-mi* after an apex - (Solo piano's repeated turn-like phrase at *poco piu mosso: piu tranquillo*, also its similarity to themes from *Irmelin* and the *Cello Sonata*)

Perhaps the work in which most of Delius's favorite Afro-American elements are found would seem to be an unlikely one, namely the 1930 orchestral work *A Song of Summer*; I say unlikely because of FD's comments to Eric Fenby prior to working on the piece:

*I want you to imagine that we are sitting on the cliffs in the heather looking over the sea. The sustained chords in the high strings suggest the clear sky, and the stillness and calmness of the scene, 7/4 in a bar (four and a three).*102

In other words we have an orchestral work from the Nordic part of the Delian psyche; there are no cliffs in Florida. Nonetheless I think it should be borne in mind that this was a reworking of another autobiographical work of 1918, *A Poem of Life and Love*. I have already noted that near the end of his life, FD seemed to be drawn to music heard in his youthful, Florida years. The resulting conflict between his comments prior to composing this piece, together with the title and subject matter of the original work, do seem to be at variance. Whichever way the reader decides to solve this problem, there is no doubt that this work contains the very essence of FD's creative output and as a result does contain almost every Delian compositional technique and idiosyncrasy:

i)   the opening pitches on the first violins [210], *mi-re-sol*, (a transposition of the *sol-la-do* unit), followed by a dying fall through the blues fifth, down to the third.

ii) the opening bass figure [104], starts with the sharpened fourth moving upwards to the dominant, is part of the blues dominant complex, followed by a jump up to the tonic and turning stepwise down to the flattened seventh; another blue note.

iii) the falling snap-note fragment preceded by a sixteenth-note scale run, played by the flute in measure 5 [105]. I feel that the use of the sharpened fourth in the opening beat of this motive is one of the few Norwegian elements in this piece; the Lydian mode is rare in Black-American music, although it is found in the spiritual *God is a God* [40].

iv) the *sol-la-mi sol* horn turn [106] is of the classic *Follow the Drinking Gourd* type, discussed in section 51.

v)   the subsidiary oboe theme at measure 18 [212] opening with an eighth note passing tone and escape-note using pentatonic intervals and then dying through the sharpened and flattened leading tone blues-complex.

vi) finally, the eight measure pentatonic melody in quadruple time using three snaps and an elongated anacrucis, found for the first time in measure 39 [36], and later almost continuously from 116 until the close. It falls very much into the anacrusis/snap group of melodies discussed in section 58. The tumbling second four-measure phrase is very Afro-American and gives it a strong similarity to the melody from the slow section of the *Violin Concerto* [35].

I am not suggesting that Delius was consciously using Afro-American devices in a piece descriptive of a Norwegian or Yorkshire seascape, but rather I feel that the Norwegian Lydian scale together with multiple Afro-American devices had entered totally into his subconscious and into the final Delian style. It is important to realize that a totally crippled and blind sixty-seven year old composer, who was used to composing at the keyboard, was forced by circumstances to reduce his musical idiom right down to its fundamentals. Here we have the very essence of Delius given to the world through the selfless dedication of the young Eric Fenby.

Mentioned in:

31   The Afro-American snap-rhythm - (Violin I's F sharp minor march-like theme at measure 48)

39   Repeated notes - (March theme at measure 48)

41   Cadence Patterns - (Cadence of the march theme at measures 51 and 55, also the woodwind/strings *sol-la-do* motive in measure 77)

45   A held note followed by multiple short notes - (Flute/oboe phrase at measure 25)

46   A held note preceded by multiple short notes - (Flute's 'seagull' motive in measure 5, also the horn's turn in measure 6)

51   Delian turn III - *sol-la-mi sol* or *sol-mi-la sol* - (Flute/oboe turn at measure 24)

55   Sixteenth-note ornaments - (Sixteenth-note upward rush at the start of the flute's 'seagull' theme in measure 5)

58   Group II: Anacrusis/snap tunes - (March theme at measure 48)

66   Group VIIb: Descending phrase using *do-te-sol* after an apex - (Reappearance of Afro-American stylings in later works)

105 Songs of Farewell [1930]

As with each of the final works written with Eric Fenby's assistance, this set of choral songs contains several motives inspired by FD's days in Florida and Virginia. In the fourth measure of the first song, the oboe plays the soaring triplet figure [121] from *A Village Romeo and Juliet,* discussed in section 54, and the flutes answer at the end of the measure with a development of the unit. Five measures later at cue 10 the clarinet plays the triplet figure a whole step lower, and other woodwind instruments play the unit a further twice at twelve-measure intervals. Repetitions of a tonally inverted, tumbling form of the flutes's answering phrase [214] become used as a ritornello between sections of the song. This tumbling form descends in thirds, *sol-mi-do la,* and pauses each time on *la* which is supported by a tonic chord. By now the pronounced use of the sixth scale degree has almost lost all of its Afro-Americaness becoming a singularly important part of FD's melodic and harmonic language. It is the importance given to the sixth scale degree which becomes almost a binding factor between these five songs; for example the orchestra's first chord [213] is a *D* major tonic chord with *B (la)* in the top voice. The soprano's opening pitches are *do* (2 beats), *la* (3, 1 & 2 beats) and *do* (2 beats); this strong use of modal scale degrees is inclined to cause an element of uncertainty as to whether *do* or *la* is the tonal center. It is a very common characteristic in pentatonic music. The prevalence of *la* as part of the tonic chord becomes even more marked commencing two measures before cue 15 where for four measures *la* is always sounding as part of the underlying chord; this use of the added-sixth has already been mentioned in section 43: *The importance of 'la'*. In Song II, *la* becomes an important degree in the cello's three-measure arpeggiated obbligato figure [149], while in measure 3 the song's first use of harmony [215] consists of the progression I, iv, I, V7 (with flattened 5th)/IV resolving on to I with an added second. Later in measures 65 to 68 *la* is always present as part of the tonic chord.

'Blue' flattened sevenths and fifths are present in the above mentioned secondary dominant chord, and later flattened sevenths and thirds are to be found in measures 69 & 70 [216] which resolve onto the tonic major chord. The soprano voices enters *mi* (anacrusis) *la* over a tonic chordal pedal; similar examples exist in each of the remaining songs.

Mentioned in:

43   The importance of *la* - (General weighting effect)

54   Delian soaring-triplet: *sol-la-do-sol* - (Oboe's triplet figure in measure 4)

59   Group III: Cakewalk rhythm in the first measure of a theme - (Cello's pentatonic obbligato figure at the opening of Song II)

This the last of FD's sonatas is another one of FD's works which owes much to the Florida and Virginia years. The opening movement's bridge theme at measure 19 [217], with its opening slow drop of a minor third and a joining lower escape note triplet figure, is repeated for emphasis in different keys for a total of eleven bars; the phrase contains the whole Afro-American experience in a single interval. This leads into the beautiful second subject in *D* [5], 6/4 with a double sarabande rhythm which I feel is FD's 3/4 version of the cakewalk unit. This melody is almost totally pentatonic with just one note, an eighth note lower neighbor *C sharp* foreign to the scale. FD finishes the melody on the opening third pitch (*F sharp*) but which the piano harmonizes with a pianissimo *B* minor chord. This melody is perhaps both too repetitive rhythmically and too sophisticated melodically to be a spiritual or work song, but again the very cell structure seems to come from Solana Grove; *mi mi-sol mi-re la*. It is possible that the nuclear theme for this melody came from the riverboat song *John Gilbert is the boat*; the similarity is illustrated clearly in example 218. The last note of the phrase is different. Perhaps poetic license, jumping down a fourth to *la* instead of moving down by step to *do,* is certainly far more expressive; the minor third is again very important here: *F sharp* up to *A.*

In the second movement we have a short-lived blue note (*G sharp* to *A*) in the opening measure of this *scherzando* movement [219]. The Trio section contains one of FD's slow dotted-note melodies; the opening phrase commencing with an anacrusis and closing with a snap unit [142] already discussed in section 58. The final movement also has another unit already discussed, namely the phrase at the opening [37] with its link to the opening theme from *Irmelin* and to themes from the *Cello Sonata* as seen in composite examples 76, 155 and 205. FD chooses to close the sonata with this gentle unassuming utterance.

Mentioned in:

21 Notated and recorded choral harmony from the 1880s and '90s - (Harmony of second subject, measure 34)

23 Traditional harmonic analysis of FD's chromatic music - (Second subject at measure 34)

29 The cakewalk rhythm - (3/4 adaption of cakewalk rhythm at measure 31)

32 Anhemitonic pentatonic scale - (Second subject at measure 34, also the violin's *lento* introduction to the final movement)

39 Repeated notes - (Second subject at measure 34, also the march-like melody from the trio section of the second movement at measure 29)

58 Group II: Anacrusis/snap tunes - (Trio section of the second movement)

63 Group Vc: Ornamented slow cakewalk rhythm in the second measure preceded by various rhythms - (Violin's slow opening of the final movement)

65 Group VIIa: Descending phrases using *la-sol-mi* after an apex - (Slow introduction to the final movement)

66 Group VIIb: Descending phrase using *do-te-sol* after an apex - (Phrase shape of the piano's opening of the final movement)

66 Group VIIb: Descending phrase using *do-te-sol* after an apex - (Reappearance of Afro-American stylings in later works)

67 Group VIII: Descending phrase using *do-la-sol* after an apex - (Similarity of the opening of the final movement to themes from *Irmelin* and the *Cello Sonata*)

107 Caprice and Elegy [1930]

Like the *Air and Dance*, this cello and chamber orchestra work is a coupling of two miniatures. The cello part of the *Caprice* [220] uses of the same basic rhythmic unit throughout, the only difference being the length of the fifth note, sometimes one beat, sometimes two; on two occasions the third beat consists of a repetition of the pitches and rhythm found on the second. Beats one and two consist of a sixteenth note and dotted eighth note followed by dotted eighth and a sixteenth note (Unit X). This identical unit is also found in the piano introduction of *I-Brasil* [27], *A Song of Summer* [36], the slow movement melody from the *Violin Concerto* [35] and in the march-like climatic melody from the final movement of the *North Country Sketches* at *very rhythmically and march-like and sustained - not quick* [197]. These motives could well have originated from the spiritual *Oh, religion is a fortune* [31]

The *Elegy* contains a striking blue note *F*, in the second measure of the B minor slow march theme at measure 17 [221]. The work's final cadence is also very memorable consisting of an enriched version of the popular blues cadence V7/ flattened VII to I; FD uses a dominant ninth on the first chord and adds a sixth to the tonic chord. The cadence is repeated with variation three times [222].

108 Idyll (Prelude and Idyll) [1930-32]

Another reworking of material written in earlier years, this time chosen mainly from the 1901/2 opera *Margot la Rouge*. The *Idyll* contains its fair share of Afro-American inspired stylings together with motives found in *A Village Romeo and Juliet* written between 1900 and 1901.

Mentioned in:
29 The cakewalk rhythm - (Flute's *A Village Romeo and Juliet* soaring theme at five measures after cue 5)
33 Mixolydian and other modes - (Violin I's *fi-sol* cadence at close of the *Prelude*)
46 A held note preceded by multiple short-notes - (Flute's soaring theme at five measures after cue 5)
52 Delian-turn IV: *sol-la-do-la* - (Violin's turn-like phrase at *piu lento* six measures before cue 7)
54 Delian soaring triplet - *sol-la-do-sol* - (Flute's soaring theme at five measures after cue 5)
55 Sixteenth-note ornaments - (Clarinet's phrase at cue 2 *poco piu mosso*)
60 Group IV: Ornamented cakewalk rhythm in the first measure of a theme - (Flute's soaring theme five measures after cue 5)

EPILOGUE

109 In the Evening by the Moonlight

By a curious coincidence, in 1880, the very well-known Afro-American black-faced minstrel performer and composer James Bland (1854-1911) composer of *Carry me back to Old Virginny* and *Oh, dem golden slippers*, composed one of his most popular songs *In the Evening by the Moonlight* [223] which parallels FD's Florida experience, but in terms of popular music.[103]

In the evening by the moonlight you could hear the old folks singing;
In the evening by the moonlight you could hear those banjos ringing;
How the old folks would enjoy it, they would sit all night and listen
As we sang in the evening by the moonlight.
How the old folks, etc.,

Bland went to Europe with Haverly's Genuine Colored Minstrels in 1881 but stayed on when the troupe returned home. I can find no use of this melody in any of FD's works, but one thing of interest is that each one of the long lines begins with an anacrucis and closes with a snap. The song is still sung today, being a favourite of barbershop groups.

MUSICAL EXAMPLES

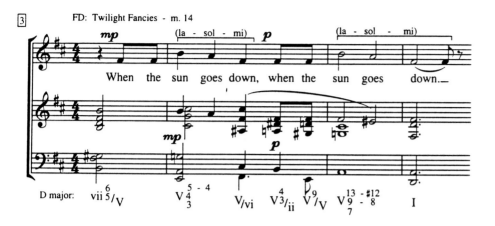

3 FD: Twilight Fancies - m. 14

When the sun goes down, when the sun goes down.

D major: vii⁶₅/V   V⁴₃⁵⁻⁴   V/vi   V⁴₃/ii   V⁹₇/V   V¹³₉⁻#¹²₈   I

4 Spiritual: Listen to de Lambs (Fenner)   [D flat chord borrowed from F minor]

Listen to de lambs cry -in',
cry' in';___ all a-cry -in', I want

F major: vi   IV   vi/i   ii⁴₃/i   I⁶₄

5 FD: Violin Sonata III - mvt. I - m. 34

[Sarabande rhythm - pentatonic melody]

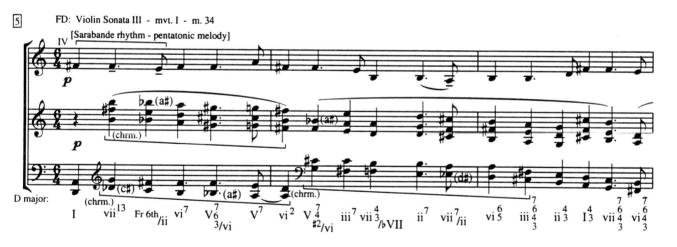

D major: I   vii¹³   Fr 6th/ii   vi⁷   V⁷₆/vi ³   V⁷   vi²   V⁴#²/vi   iii⁷   vii⁷₃/bVII   ii⁷   vii⁷/ii   vi⁶₅   iii⁶₄₃   ii⁴₃   I³₄   vii⁷₆₃   vi⁷₄₃

iii²   vi⁶₅   vi⁴₃   V₃   vi⁴₃   ii⁶₅

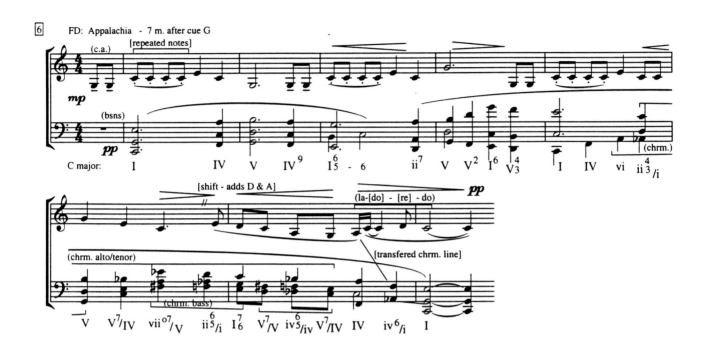

6 FD: Appalachia - 7 m. after cue G

[repeated notes]

(c.a.)

mp

(bsns)

pp

C major: I   IV   V   IV⁹   I⁶₅ - 6   ii⁷   V   V²   I⁶   V⁴₃   I   IV   vi   ii⁴₃/i

[shift - adds D & A]

(la-[do] - [re] - do)

pp

(chrm. alto/tenor)

[transfered chrm. line]

(chrm. bass)

V   V⁷/IV   vii°⁷/V   ii⁶₅/i   I⁷₆   V⁷/V   iv⁶₅/iv   V⁷/IV   IV   iv⁶/i   I

7 Work song/Spiritual: I need another witness for my Lord

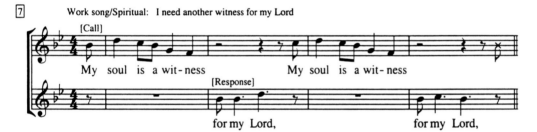

[Call]

My soul is a wit-ness   My soul is a wit-ness

[Response]

for my Lord,   for my Lord,

8 FD: Florida - Sunset (Danza)

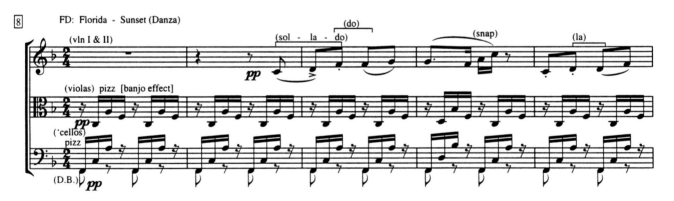

(vln I & II)

(sol - la - do)   (do)   (snap)   (la)

pp

(violas) pizz [banjo effect]

pp

('cellos)
pizz

(D.B.) pp

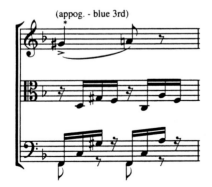

(appog. - blue 3rd)

76

17 Spiritual: Gabriel's Trumpet

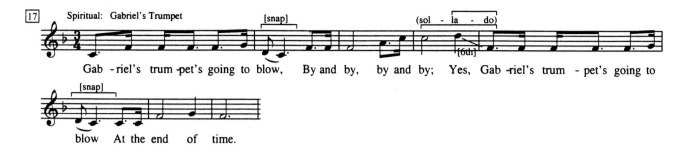

Gab - riel's trum -pet's going to blow, By and by, by and by; Yes, Gab -riel's trum - pet's going to

blow At the end of time.

18 FD: The Walk to the Paradise Garden - opening

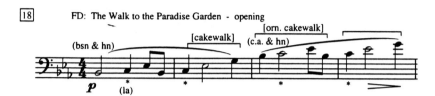

19 FD: Idyll - 5 m. after cue 5

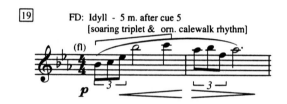

20 FD: Koanga - Act I - cue 26

Pa he said 'Son, you done grieve your Ma's mind, Must you wed that Phil- is-tine wo -man?

21 Cakewalk rhythm   real 3/4 adaption   Delius's 3/4 adaption [Sarabande]

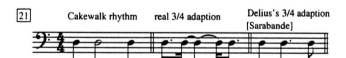

22 FD: Cello Concerto - m. 290

23 FD: Irmelin - Act II - m.231

24 Spiritual: Steal away to Jesus

Steal away, Steal away, Steal away to Je -sus. Steal away, steal a -way home,

78

25 **Spiritual: Sometimes I feel like a motherless child**

[cakewalk]

Some -times I feel like a mother -less child, Some -times I feel like a mother -less child,

26 **African Counting Song**

Nin - ni non - no - si -mun gi, nin - ni non - no al -mun gi, nin - ni non - no (etc.)

27 **FD: I-Brasil - opening**

[snap] [unit X]

There's sor-row on the wind, my grief, (etc.)

[unit X]

mp [snap]

(etc.)

28 **FD: Air and Dance - opening [dotted-note melody]**

p

29 **Folk ballad: The Lonesome Road [dotted-note melody]**

Look down, look down that lone - some road,__ Hang down yo' head an' cry.

30 **Animal Song: La Pluie Tombe [dotted-note melody]**

La pluie tom - be, Cra -peau chan - te, Oin, oin! oin, oin! oin, oin!__M'a pa -le baigner moin.

31 **Spiritual: Oh, Religion is a Fortune**

[Unit X] [cakewalk] (la) [unit X] [cakewalk]
[snap] [snap]

Oh, re - lig -ion is a for -tune, I really do be -lieve Oh, re -lig-ion is a for -tune, I (etc)

32 **Rowing Song: Lay this body down**

(me - do)
[snap]

O grave -yard, O grave - yard,__ I'm walk -in' troo de grave- yard; Lay dis bo-dy down,

33 Spiritual: Rise, Mourners

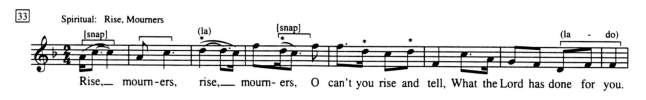

Rise,— mourn-ers, rise,— mourn-ers, O can't you rise and tell, What the Lord has done for you.

34 Gaelic Lament: Cumha Aonchuis

Ho ro's na hu o, falbh o o— ro n'aill u, ho— ro 'sna hu o.

35 FD: Violin Concerto - cue 19 [pentatonic tumbling melody]

36 FD: A Song of Summer - m. 48

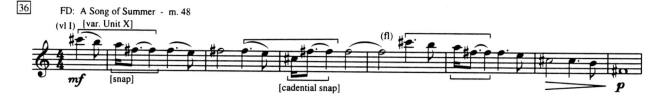

37 FD: Violin Sonata III - mvt. III - opening
[E minor pent.]

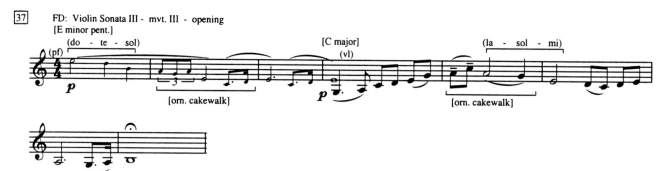

38 FD: Piano Concerto - opening

39 FD: Songs of Sunset - 3 m. before cue 30

(c.a.) *p*

Country Blues (Florida): I been a bad, bad girl [Key: F Locrian pentatonic mode]

I been a bad,_____ bad girl,_____

40 Spiritual: God is a God!
[Key; C Lydian mode]

(fi)

God is a God! God don't nev - er change! God is a God_____ An' He

al -ways will be God!

41 FD: Dance Rhapsody I - cue 2 [* Lydian mode]
[Key: A Lydian mode]

(ob) (fi)

mf

42 FD: Idyll - 4 m. before close of the Prelude

[Key: E]   [sharpened fourth]

(fi)

(vl I)

pp   *ppp*

43 Spiritual: In this Lan'
[Key: E flat minor]   [E flat major]

Lord help the po' and the need- y, In this lan' Inthis lan'Lord help the po' and the need y, In this

lan'. (etc)

44 Work song: Jim Strange killed Lula
[Pentatonic tumbling phrase]

Let me tell you_ Ba- by_____ Let me tell you right_____

45 FD: Florida - Daybreak - 7 m. after cue 3
(vls I & II) [tumbling phrase]

mp

46 FD: Koanga - Act I - 8 m. before cue 6
[Pentatonic tumbling phrase]

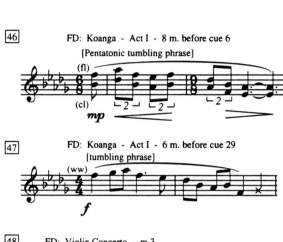

47 FD: Koanga - Act I - 6 m. before cue 29
[tumbling phrase]

48 FD: Violin Concerto - m.3
[tumbling phrase]   [angular 16th note ornament]

49 FD: String Quartet - close of mvt 1
(vl I) [tumbling phrase]   [blue note]   [cadential snap]

50 Work song: John Henry
[arch-shaped phrases with limited note set]

This ol' ham-mer   killed John Hen-ry!   This ol' ham-mer   killed John Hen-ry!   This ol'

ham-mer   killed John Hen-ry,   But this ol' ham-mer   won't kill me!

51 Spiritual: There's a meeting here tonight
Come a-long

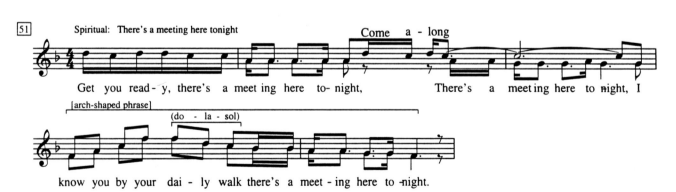

Get you read-y, there's a meet-ing here to-night,   There's a meet-ing here to-night, I

[arch-shaped phrase]
(do - la - sol)

know you by your dai-ly walk there's a meet-ing here to-night.

52 FD: Irmelin - opening
[arch-shaped phrase]

pp   (do - te - sol)

83

C [from opening theme]

[tumbling phrase]

mf

59 FD: Double Concerto - cue 18 ['Sing to Mary']

[inverted arch-shaped phrases]   [shift] [arch-shaped phrase]   [shift]

(solo cello)
p espress.

60 Work song: Seben times [call and response]
[limited note set]

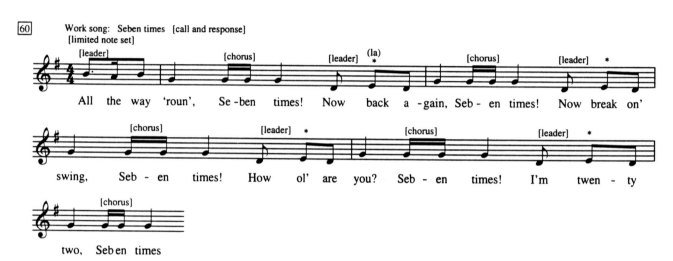

[leader]   [chorus]   [leader] (la)   [chorus]   [leader] *

All the way 'roun', Se-ben times! Now back a-gain, Seb-en times! Now break on'

[chorus]   [leader] *   [chorus]   [leader] *

swing, Seb-en times! How ol' are you? Seb-en times! I'm twen-ty

[chorus]

two, Seben times

61 FD: Florida - At Night - m. 15
[limited note set: E, F sharp, A & B]

(hn)   (la)   ┌3┐   ┌3┐   (la - do)

p

62 FD: Irmelin - Act III - m. 391

(Irmelin)   [blue note]

How beau-ti-ful and si-lent all na-ture lies out there___ And the frag-rant

per fumes how they sweet-ly scent the air___ The fields and woods lie___

blush-ing in the sun's last rays and the night breeze whis-pers_ love_ long-ing and

bliss._   love long-ing and bliss.

63 FD: Irmelin - Act II - m.756

[blue note]

64 FD: The Walk to the Paradise Gardens - 5 m. after cue 1

[blue note]

(ob)

p

65 FD: Violin Concerto - cue 15

(vl solo)   [16th-note orn.] [blue note]

(Strgs)

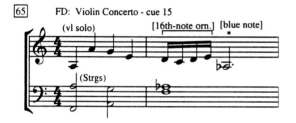

66 FD: Koanga - chorus prelude to Act II

[Many repeated notes]

(sol - mi - re / transp. do-la-sol)

[Key: A flat]   Now once in a way, We are free for a day, And can lay down our sic -kles and our hoes; Let the cane

67 FD: Koanga - Act I - cue 28

(Palmyra) [many repeated notes]   (do - le - sol)   (me - do)

I   feel a   strange for -bod -ing in my heart; this voo doo Prince will bring me to my grave.

68 Spiritual: Ride on, King Jesus - refrain

[orn. cakewalk]

(la)   *   * *   *   *   *

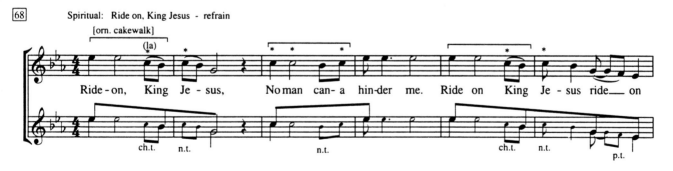

Ride - on,   King Je - sus,   No man can- a hin-der me. Ride on King Je - sus ride___ on

ch.t.   n.t.   n.t.   ch.t.   n.t.   p.t.

no man___ can- a hin-der me.

p.t.   n.t.

85

69

Spiritual: Swing low, sweet chariot
[many repeated notes]

Swing low, sweet char - i - ot,— Com - ing for to car-ry me home. Swing low, sweet char - i - ot,—

Com -ing for to car-ry me home.

70

Spiritual: Gwine up
[oscillation]

Oh,— saints an' sin ners will a you go, see de heb-ben-ly land, I'm a gwine up to heaven for to (etc.)

71

FD: Piano Concerto - cue 3

72

FD: String Quartet - Late Swallows - 2 ms. before cue 8

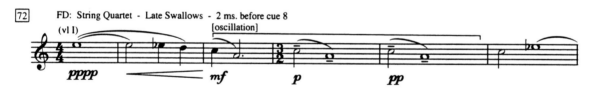

73

FD: Songs of Sunset - 4 m. before cue 41

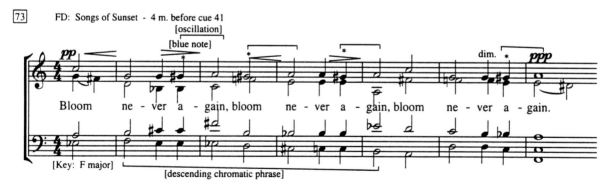

Bloom ne - ver a - gain, bloom ne - ver a - gain, bloom ne - ver a - gain.

[Key: F major]   [descending chromatic phrase]

74

FD: Dance Rhapsody I - 4 m. before cue 3

75 FD: Florida - Daybreak (La Calinda)- 4 m. before cue 8
[arch-shape phrase] (flts) [multiple snap] (la-sol-mi)
[p]

76 FD: Violin Sonata III - mvt III (opening) [see ex 37]
(do - te - sol)

Work song: Gonna leave Big Rock behind (refrain) (transp. from F) [see ex 55]
Heave ho! heave ho I'm gon-na leave Big Rock be-hind.

FD: Irmelin - opening (transp. from G sharp minor) [see ex 52]

FD: Piano Concerto - opening (transp. from C minor) [see ex 38]

FD: Irmelin - Act I - m.20 (transp. from G sharp minor) see ex 158]

77 FD: String Quartet - mvt IV - m. 10
(vl I) [osc.3rds]
mf mp p

78 Work song: Got no Money
(la - do) // [shift]
Got no mo-ney but I will have some Su-sie___ Ain't got no mo-ney but I will have some Su-sie___

// [shift] [snap] (la - do)
— Ain't got no mon-ey but I will have some Jes' you wait till pay day comes Su-sie___

79 Road Gang Song: Pick 'em up
// [shift]
Pick 'em up, pick 'em up, Let 'em fall down___ Dere's a hard rock-y

// [shift] (mi - do)
bot-tom An' she must be foun'.

87

80   Lullaby: O Mother Glasco

O Moth- er Glas- co where's yo' lamb? I left him down in de mead- ow, Birds an' de bees
sing-in' in de trees, Po' lit tle lamb say 'mam - my'.

81   FD: Cello Concerto - m. 93
[Key: D major] [pentatonic phrase]

82   FD: Piano Concerto - 3 m. after cue 3
[nuclear structure - see ex. 86, 115 & 117]

83   FD: String Quartet Mvt. IV - 4 m. before cue 3

84   FD: Koanga - Act III - 4 m. before cue 10
(Rangwan)

Voo - doo hear!   The fire con - sumes the blood! Voo-doo hear! I shed my blood for thee!
Spiritual: Great day! [see ex 91]

FD: String Quartet mvt IV (transp. from B major) [see ex 92]

FD: Koanga - close of Act III (transp. from G major) [see ex 94]

FD: Serenade from Hassan m. 2 [see ex 93]

85 FD: Cello Concerto - m. 36

[blue note]
(vl I) p

86 Work song: Screw this cotton

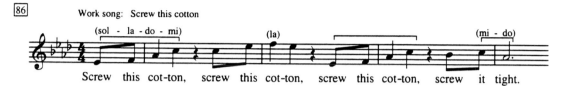
(sol - la - do - mi)   (la)   (mi - do)
Screw this cot-ton, screw this cot-ton, screw this cot-ton, screw it tight.

87 Chilfdren's Song : Short'nin' Bread - refrain

* (la)   *   *   *   *   *   (mi - re - do)
Mam-my's lit-tle ba - by loves short' -nin', short'-nin', Mam-my's lit-tle ba-by loves short' -nin' bread.

88 FD: A Village Romeo and Juliet - Scene VI - cue 84

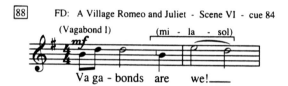
(Vagabond I) (mi - la - sol)
mf
Va ga - bonds are we!___

89 FD: Cello Concerto - m. 158
(vl I - cellos at lower octave)

[E: major]

(sol - la - do)   (la)   (la)
p

90 Spiritual: Nobody knows the trouble I've seen - [pentatonic]

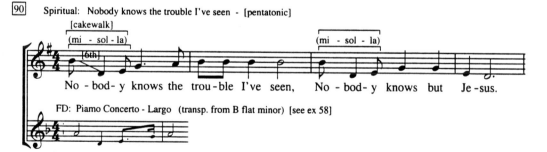
[cakewalk]
(mi - sol - la)   (mi - sol - la)
[6th]
No - bod-y knows the trou-ble I've seen, No - bod-y knows but Je -sus.

FD: Piamo Concerto - Largo (transp. from B flat minor) [see ex 58]

91 Spiritual: Great Day! - [pentatonic]

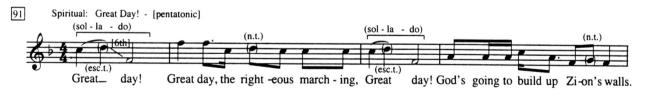
(sol - la - do)   (n.t.)   (sol - la - do)   (n.t.)
[6th]
(esc.t.)   (esc.t.)
Great_ day! Great day, the right -eous march - ing, Great   day! God's going to build up Zi -on's walls.

92 FD: String Quartet - mvt IV - 3 m. before cue 21

(vl I)   (transp. sol-la - do)
[6th]
mf   p   pp

93 FD: Serenade from Hassan - opening

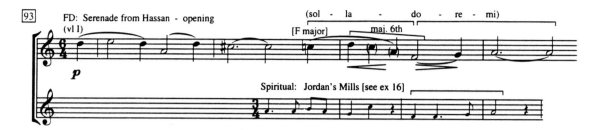

(vl I)

[F major] maj. 6th (sol - la - do - re - mi)

p

Spiritual: Jordan's Mills [see ex 16]

94 FD: Koanga - Act III - final ms.

(ob) 3 (do - la - (sol) - la - do)

[6th]

(hn)

[6th]

ff

95 Field Holler [James] - [held note followed by multiple short notes]

[blue] *fz* 3

Yuh_____ 3 3

96 Field Holler [James] [held note followed by multiple short notes]

ff *f* (sol-la - do) *fz*

Oh___ Lord, have mercy on this dyin' world.

97 FD: Mass of Life - mvt III - m. 2 [held note followed by multiple short notes]

pppp (sol - la - do)

(altos) Ah!_____

98 FD: Song of Summer - m. 24 [held note followed by multiple short notes]

(ob - fl octave higher)

[sol - la - mi -sol turn]

p 3 3

[Key: B major]

99 FD: Song of the High Hills - 3 ms. after cue 23 [held note followed by multiple short notes]

(ob)

mf 3 3

100 FD: Brigg Fair - opening [held note followed by multiple short notes]

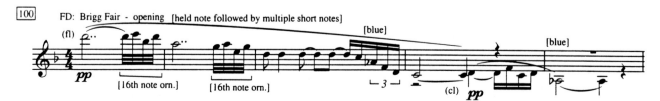

(fl) [blue] [blue]

pp

[16th note orn.] [16th note orn.] 3 (cl) *pp*

90

101 Work song: Make a Longtime Man feel bad - [Jackson]
[mult. short notes followed by a held note]

[mi - la - sol]

Ro - ber- ta,___ let_your hair grow long, let it grow

102 Buttermilk Cry [Kennedy] [mult. short notes followed by a held note]

[blue note]

But - ter - milk_____ But - ter - milk_____

103 FD: Sea Drift - cue 3 [mult. short notes followed by a held note]

[sol-la-mi sol turn]

(ob) ⌐ 3 ⌐
p

104 FD: A Song of Summer - opening [mult. short notes followed by a held note]
(cellos & d.b)

[trans. mi - la - sol]

pp

105 FD: A Song of Summer - m. 5 [mult. short notes followed by a held note]

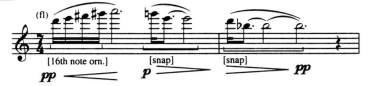

(fl)

[16th note orn.]   [snap]   [snap]
pp   p   pp

106 FD: Violin Sonata II - Piu tranquillo e piu lento [mult. short notes followed by a held note]

[ff]
[variant sol-la-mi turn]   [sol-la-mi turn]   p [sol-la-mi turn]

107 River-boat Sounding [Wheeler]

And it's Quar - ter Less Fo'._____

108 Two River-boat Soundings [Wheeler]

Quar - ter Ta - ree. Mark___ Ta - wain.

109a   Grieg: En Svane - m. 9

109b   FD: Summer Evening - opening
[mi-sol-la-mi turn]   ['En Svane' rhythm]

110   Grieg: Evening in the Mountains, op 68 - m. 23
[la - sol - me turn]

111   FD: Koanga - Act II - 8 ms. before cue 7
[la-sol-me turn]

a man to call my own,

112   FD: On Hearing the First Cuckoo in Spring - m.2
[la-sol-me turn]

113   FD: North Country Sketches - Autumn - 1 m. before cue 5
(fl & ob an octave lower)
[sol-la-mi-sol turn]

114   FD: The Song of the High Hills - 1 m. after cue 3
(fl/ob.cl/vl II/.cello)
[sol-la-me-sol turn]   [chrom. sol-la-me-sol turn]

115   FD: Koanga -Act III - 7 m. after cue 13
(vl)   [sol-la-do-la turn]

116   FD: Idyll - 6 m. before cue 7
[sol-la-do-la turn]
(vl I)

134 Religious Song: There's a man goin' round taking names - m. 5

O he took my mother's name an' he left my heart in pain O— there's a man go-in' round tak in' names

135 FD: Irmelin - Act III - m. 42

136 FD: In a Summer Garden - m. 6

137 Mendelssohn (adpt. Cummings): Hark! the herald angels sing

138 Song: Possum up a Gum Tree - (notd. Mathews)

Pos-sum up a Gum Tree Up he go up he go Ra-coon in the hol-low Down be -low down be -low Him pull

139 FD: Florida - Sunset - Danza [see ex 8]

FD: Mass of Life - mvt. III - cue 19 (note values halved) [see ex 15]

FD: Two Part Songs - II (transp. from D major) [see ex 54]

FD: String Quartet - mvt. IV - 4 ms. before cue 3 (trsp. from B flat & note-values halved) [see ex 83]

FD: The Song of the High Hills - 1 m. before cue 31 (transp. from E minor)

FD: Irmelin - Act III - m. 42 - note values halved (transp. from E flat) [see ex 135]

FD: In a Summer garden - m. 6 - note values doubled [see ex 136]

145   Hymn/Spiritual: The Morning Trumpet

You may bu-ry me in the East, You may bu-ry me in the West, But I'll hear the trum-pet

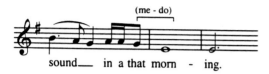

sound___ in a that morn - ing.

146   FD: The Walk to the Paradise Garden - cue15

147   FD: Violin Concerto - opening

148   FD: Florida - Daybreak - 1 m. before cue 2

149   FD: Songs of Farewell - mvt. II - opening

150   FD: Requiem - mvt.III - 1 m. before cue 25

151   FD: A Village Romeo and Juliet - Act I - 3 m. after cue 5

158 FD: Irmelin - Act I - m. 20

(do - te - sol)

p

[orn. cakewalk]

159 FD: Dance Rhapsody No. 2 - m.1

(fl)

p

(la - do)

160 FD: Dance Rhapsody No.m. 147

(ob)

p

[3/4 'cakewalk']

161 River-Song: I'm goin' up the rivah

[orn. cakewalk]   [cakewalk]   [orn. cakewalk]   [snap]

I'm go-in' up the riv-uh, An' I won't stay long,— I'll have plen ty mon - ey When the boat gits back.

162 Travel song: Follow the Drinkin' Gourd

[cakewalk variant]   (sol-la-me-sol turn transposed)

Fol- low_____ the drink - in' gourd!   Fol- low_____ the drin -kin' gourd

Alternative reading (D.H.)

163 Spiritual: Stand on a Sea of Glass

[cakewalk] [variant cakewalk]   [var. cakewalk]   [cakewalk]   [var. cakewalk]   [cakewalk]   (me - do)

O___ dis un- i-on! Sing dis un- i-on! I love dis_ un- i-on, Stand on a sea of glass. (etc.)

164 Spiritual: Big Camp Meeting in the Promised Land

[variant cakewalk]

O dis un- i-on! O dis un- i-on band!_ O dis un- i-on! (etc.)

165 Spiritual: There is a Balm in Gilead

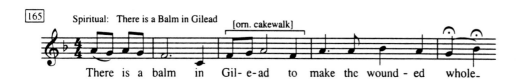

[orn. cakewalk]

There is a balm in Gil- e-ad to make the wound - ed whole_

100

166 FD: Koanga - Act II - 12 m. before cue 3
(chorus)

mp

He will meet her when the sun goes down, When the whip -poor -will sings to the moon

FD: Appalachia - 7 m. after cue G (transp. from C) [see ex 6]

(c.a.)

FD: Irmelin - Act I - m. 135 (transp. from B - note values halved) [see ex 182]

(A Maid)

167 Roustabout Song: Boatman Dance, Boatman sing
(transp. la - sol - mi)

Heigh - ho boat -man row, Sail-in' down de riv-uh on de O - hi - o,—

168 Black-faced Minstrel Song: De Boatman Dance
(transp. la - sol - mi) (mi-do)

Heigh O, de boat -man row, Float - in down de rib- er de O- hi- o.

169 FD: Violin Sonata II - Poco meno mosso
(la-sol-mi)

(pf) *mf* 3

170 Spiritual: I'm agoing to join the band
(do-te-sol)
Hal- le lu— jah!—

I'm a going to join the band, I'm a going to join the band,

171 Spiritual: We are climbing Jacob's Ladder
(do-la-sol)

We are— climb- ing— Ja - cob's— lad-der

172 FD: Irmelin - Act I Prelude - closing (m. 44)
(do - la - sol)

p

173 FD: Irmelin - Act IV - m. 1044
(Nils) (do - la - sol)

Fare thee well Oh! sweet sil-ver stream.

174   FD: Cello Concerto - m. 185

(do - la - sol)

(solo cello)
mp

175   FD: Cello Concerto - m. 277

(do - la - sol)

(fl/vl I & II)
f   *p*

176   FD: Cello Sonata - m. 25

(transp. do - la - sol)

(solo cello)
mp

177   FD: Florida - Sunset - cue 4

(ob)   (transp. sol-la-do)

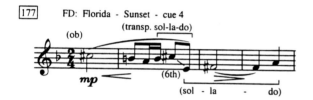

mp
(6th)
(sol - la - do)

178   FD: Koanga - Prologue - 11 ms. after cue 2

(cellos)   (transp. sol -la - do)

pp
(6th)
(sol - la - do)

Henry C. Work: Marching through Georgia

Bring the good old bu - gle, boys! we'll sing an-oth-er song -

179   FD: String Quartet - Late Swallows - 6 ms. after cue 4

(vl I)   (transp. sol -la-do)   (la - do)

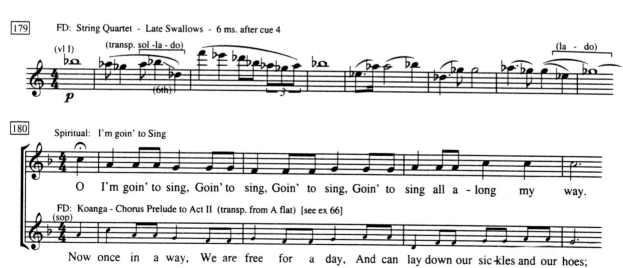

p
(6th)

180   Spiritual: I'm goin' to Sing

O I'm goin' to sing, Goin' to sing, Goin' to sing, Goin' to sing all a - long my way.

FD: Koanga - Chorus Prelude to Act II (transp. from A flat) [see ex 66]
(sop)

Now once in a way, We are free for a day, And can lay down our sic-kles and our hoes;

188   FD: Songs of Sunset - 6 m. after cue 4

(do - te - [do] - sol)

189   FD: Songs of Sunset - cue 15

(do - la - sol)

(fl & ob in octaves)

190   FD: Songs of Sunset - closing
(chorus & strings)

(la - [re] - do)

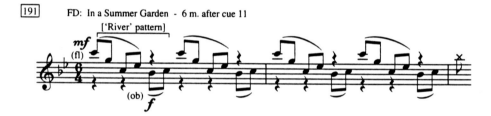

dream,   dream.

191   FD: In a Summer Garden - 6 m. after cue 11

['River' pattern]

(fl)

(ob)

192   Dance Song: Jump Jim Crow

(do - la - sol)   (mi - re - do)

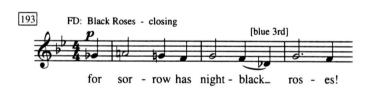

Turn about and twist about, And do jis' so, An' every time you turn a-bout, You jump Jim Crow

193   FD: Black Roses - closing

[blue 3rd]

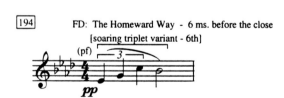

for sor - row has night - black_ ros - es!

194   FD: The Homeward Way - 6 ms. before the close

[soaring triplet variant - 6th]

(pf)

195   FD: The Homeward Way - 4 ms. before the close

[blue 7th]

on my home -ward jour - ney,

104

196 FD: The Homeward Way - closing 2 ms.

197 FD: North Country Sketches - The March of Spring - 4 ms. after cue 53

198 FD: North Country Sketches - Dance - cue 25

199 FD: North Country Sketches - Winter Landscape - 3 ms. after cue 19

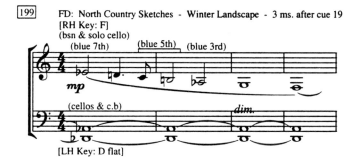

200 FD: Requiem - mvt. III

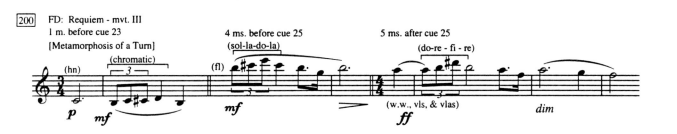

201 FD: Air and Dance - m. 14 of the Dance

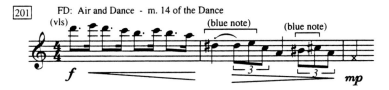

206

FD: String Quartet - opening Mvt. II
(vl I) (me-do)
mp

Work Song: John Henry [see ex 50]

FD: String Quartet - mvt I (transp. from E minor) [see ex 49]

207

Fiddle Tune: Roaring River (Red River Plantation c. 1853)
(sol - la - do) [16th note orn.] [16th note orn.] (sol - la - do)

208

FD: Cello Concerto m. 290 (transp. 8va sopra) [see ex 22]

Spiritual: Ma Soul's Determin' [transp. from C]
Oh, ma lit-tle soul, soul's de - ter - min'   Oh, ma lit-tle soul,   soul's de-ter-min'

Water cry (James) (transp. from C) [see ex 133]

FD: Intermezzo from 'Hassan' - m. 5
[orn. cakewalk]   (sol-do-la-sol)
(cl)   3
p

FD: Violin Sonata I - Slow (transp. from G) [see ex 203]
(vl)
p
[orn. cakewalk]   [cakewalk]

209 FD: Violin Sonata II - 2 ms. after poco meno mosso
[tumbling phrase]
(vl)
mf

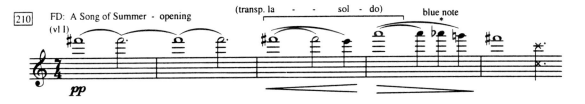

210 FD: A Song of Summer - opening
(transp. la - - sol - do)   blue note
(vl I)   *
pp

211 FD: A Song of Summer - m. 6

212 FD: A Song of Summer - m. 18

213 FD: Songs of Farewell - opening

How   sweet   the   si - lent

214 FD: Songs of Farewell - no. I - m. 4

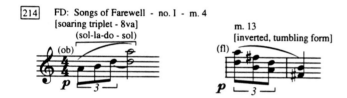

215 FD: Songs of Farewell - no. II - m. 3

216 FD: Songs of Farewell - II - m. 69

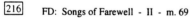

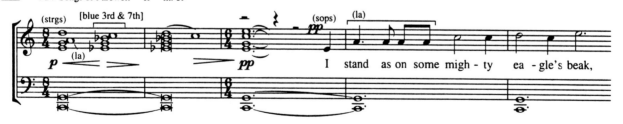

I   stand   as on some migh - ty   ea - gle's beak,

217 FD: Violin Sonata III - m. 19

218 FD: Violin Sonata III - mvt. I - m. 34 [see ex 5]

(mi - mi - sol - mi - re [do])

River boat song: John Gilbert

(mi - mi - sol - mi - re - [do])

John Gil - bert is the boat,

219 FD: Violin Sonata III - mvt. II - opening

(vl)   [blue note]

220 FD: Cello Caprice - m. 6

[rhythmic unit X]

(cello)

221 FD: Cello Elegy - m. 17

(cello)   (do - te - sol)

(blue note)

222 FD: Cello Elegy - closing

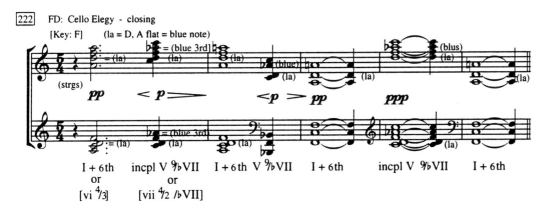

[Key: F]   (la = D, A flat = blue note)

(strgs)

I + 6th   incpl V ⁹/♭VII   I + 6th   V ⁹/♭VII   I + 6th   incpl V ⁹/♭VII   I + 6th
or   or
[vi ⁴/3]   [vii ⁴/2 /♭VII]

223 James Bland - In the Evening by the Moonlight

[anacrusis]   [snap]

In the eve -ning by the moon - light you could hear the old folks sing - ing, In the

[snap]

eve -ning by the moon - light you could hear those ban - jos ring -ing; How the

Notes

Preface

1 Eric Fenby as Guest Speaker at the 1981 Jacksonville Delius Festival when answering a question 'from the floor' on the presence of Afro-American musical influence and melodies in the music of FD.

1 Early Years

2 Clare Delius, *Frederick Delius: Memories of My Brother* (London: I. Nicholson & Watson, 1935), p. 45.

3 Gloria Jahoda, *The Road to Samarkand* (New York: Charles Scribner's Sons, 1969), pp. 21-22.

2 FD in Florida

4 William Randel, 'Delius in America,' *The Virginia magazine of History and Biography,* July 1971, repr. in Christopher Redwood, *A Delius Companion* (London: John Calder, 1976), p. 152.

5 FD's letter to Elgar of January 4th, 1934, quoted by Lionel Carley and Robert Threlfall in *Delius: A Life in Pictures* (London: Oxford University Press, 1977), p. 12.

6 *But he do for hisself mostly .....* (Julia Sanks), Gloria Jahoda, *The Other Florida* (New York: Charles Scribner's Sons, 1967), p. 267.

7 Philip Heseltine [Peter Warlock] and Hubert Foss, *Frederick Delius,* 1923 (London: The Bodley Head, 1950), p. 146.

8 *The Road to Samarkand,* (Jahoda) pp. 63-64.

3 Leaves Florida for Virginia, New York and Leipzig

9 'Delius in America,' (Redwood) p. 152.

10 Percy Grainger, 'The Personality of Frederick Delius,' *The Australian Musical News,* July 1934, repr. in Christopher Redwood, *A Delius Companion* (London: John Calder, 1976), pp. 117 & 122.

11 Tasmin Little, *The Lost Child,* (Video) - reviewed in *The Delian,* April 1999, Philadelphia, p. 9.

12 *The Other Florida,* (Jahoda) p. 259.

4 Florida in retrospect

13 *Frederick Delius,* (Warlock & Foss) p. 145.

14 *Now let's clear the air .....* (FD), Eric Fenby: *Delius as I knew him* (London: G. Bell & Sons, 1936. repr. Faber and Faber, 1981). p. 25.

15 Sir Thomas Beecham, *Frederick Delius* (London: Hutchinson & Co., 1959), pp. 33-34.

16 *Frederick Delius,* (Warlock & Foss) p. 145.

17 *Delius: a Life in Pictures,* (Carley & Threlfall) p. 12.

18 *and said he owed ......* 'Delius, the Composer Dead', London: *Daily Mirror.* June 11th. 1934.

19 *After lunch one day ....* *Frederick Delius,* (Beecham) p. 82.

5 European influences

20 *Delius as I knew him,* (Fenby) p. 209.

21 *Delius: A Life in Pictures,* (Carley & Threlfall) p. 6.

22 'The Personality of Frederick Delius,' (Redwood) p. 127.

23 *Delius as I knew him,* (Fenby) p. 209.

24   'The Personality of Frederick Delius,' (Redwood) p. 119.
25   *There is a tendency* .... (Harry T. Burleigh),   Louis Biancolli and William S. Mann *The Analytical Concert Guide* (London: Cassell & Company Ltd., 1957), pp. 214-215.
26   'The Personality of Frederick Delius,' (Redwood) pp. 120-121.

8   River (rowing) songs
27   William Francis Allen, Charles Pickard Ware and Lucy McKim Garrison, *Slave Songs of the United States* (New York: A. Simpson, 1867), quoting W. H. Russell of the London Times 'My Diary North and South,' p. 19.
28   James Hungerford, 'The Old Plantation.,' (New York: Harper and Brothers, 1859), repr, in Eileen Southern *Readings in Black American Music* (New York: W, W, Norton, 1971), pp. 71-81.
29   *De boat songs*........ Ibid, (Southern), p. 73.

10   Meter in African and Afro-American song and dance
30   George Washington Cable, 'The Dance in Place Congo' also 'Creole Slave Songs' (*The Century Magazine*, February and April, volume XXXI, 1886), repr. in Bernard Katz, *The Social Implications of Early Negro Music in the United States: with over 150 of the Songs, Many of Them with Their Music,* (New York: Arno Press, 1969), pp. 31-68.
31   A. M. Jones, *Studies of African Music,* (London: Oxford University Press, 1959), p. 28.

12   Traditional antebellum Afro-American choral singing
32   Christopher Palmer, *Delius: Portrait of a Cosmopolitan* (London: Duckworth, 1976), p. 92.
33   *There is no singing in parts* ...... *Slave Songs of the United States,* (Allen, Ware & Garrison) p. v.

13   The Revivalist and Jubilee Styles
34   Eileen Southern, *The Music of Black Americans* (New York: W. W. Norton Company, 1971), p. 259.

14   The Male Quartet
35   Lynn Abbott, ' 'Play that Barber Shop chord': A Case for the African-American Origin of Barbershop harmony,' *American Music* (Quarterly), University of Illinois, Fall 1992, pp. 280-325.
36   Vera Brodsky Lawrence, *Music for Patriots, Politicians, and Presidents* (New York: MacMillan Publishing Co., Inc., 1975), p. 128-129.
37   'Delius in America,' (Redwood), p. 152.
38   'Play that Barber Shop chord,' (Abbott) pp. 280-325.
39   James W. Johnson & J. Rosamond Johnson, *American Negro Spirituals* (New York: Viking Press, 1925 & 1926), pp. 35-36.

15   FD and blackfaced minstrels
40   *Frederick Delius: Memories of My Brother*, (C. Delius) p. 45.
41   *The Music of Black Americans,* pp. 233-238,   also Hans Nathan, *Dan Emmett and the Rise of Early Negro Minstrelsy,* (Norman: University of Oklahoma Press, 1962).
42   *Dan Emmett and the Rise of Early Negro Minstrelsy,* (Nathan) p. 159 *et seq.*
43   *Frederick Delius: Memories of My Brother*, (C. Delius) p. 45.

16   Influences - an introduction
44   *Those of Tennessee* ...... *Slave Songs of the United States,* (Allen, Ware & Garrison) pp. xix-xx.
45   *The Road to Samarkand,* (Jahoda) p. 72.
46   John Bird, *Percy Grainger* (London: Faber and Faber, 1976), pp. 129-130.

20 The influence of Afro-American choral singing on the music of FD
47 Cecil Gray, 'Memories of Delius,' *Musical Chairs* (London: Home and van Thal, 1948), repr. in Redwood, p. 140.
48 *Delius: a Life in Pictures*, (Carley & Threlfall) p. 12.
49 *Delius: Portrait of a Cosmopolitan*, (Palmer) p. 92.
50 *When we wanted to meet at night.....* B.A. Botkin, ed, 'Slave Narrative Collection,' (Washington: Library of Congress, 1941), repr. on Southern, *Readings in Black American Music*, p.121.
51 'Delius in America,' (Redwood) p. 152.
52 *Slave Songs of the United States*, (Allen, Ware & Garrison) pp. xix-xx.
53 *Frederick Delius*, (Warlock & Foss) p. 42.

21 Notated and recorded choral harmony from the 1880s and '90s
54 *Delius: Portrait of a Cosmopolitan*, (Palmer) pp. 15, 16 & 35.
55 Arthur Hutchings, *Delius - A Critical Biography* (London: MacMillan & Co. Ltd., 1948), p. 166.
56 'Memories of Delius,' (Redwood) p. 140.

22 Remembered harmony used by Black Quartets in the early 1900s
57 Sigmund Spaeth, *They Still Sing of Love* (New York: Horace Liveright, 1929) pp. 62-63, <u>also</u> 'Play That Barber Shop Chord,' (Abbott).
58 'Delius in America,' (Redwood) p. 152.
59 *About every .....* ' 'Play That Barber Shop Chord': A Case for the African-American Origin of Barbershop Harmony', (Abbott) p. 290.
60 John W. Work, *American Negro Songs* (New York: Crown Publishers, 1940), p. 46.
61 Ibid, pp. 46 & 214.

27 Banjo (m'bira) and river-influenced accompaniments.
62 *Frederick Delius*, (Beecham) p. 38.

28 Meter
63 'The Dance in Place Congo' also 'Creole Slave Songs,' (Katz) p. 31 - 68.
64 J. H. Kwabena Nketia, *The Music of Africa* (New York: W. W. Norton & Company Inc, 1974), p. 130.

38 Blue notes
65 *How beautiful and silent .....* Irmelin (London: Boosey and Hawkes, 1953), Act III, measures 391-409.
66 'The Personality of Frederick Delius,' (Redwood) pp. 117 & 122,
67 *The Lost Child - video* (Little)

41 Cadence patterns
68 'The Personality of Frederick Delius,' (Redwood) pp. 120-121.

42 The 'shift' technique
69 *The Music of Africa*, (Nketia) p. 150 *et seq.*
70 *The Road to Samarkand*, (Jahoda) p. 181.
71 Willis Laurence James, 'The Romance of the Negro Folk Cry in America,' *Phylon* (University of Atlanta), Ist, Qt. 1955.

47 Riverboat soundings
72 Mary Wheeler, *Steamboatin' Days: Folk Songs of the River Packet Era* (Baton Rouge, LA: Louisiana State University Press, 1944), pp. 59-66.

48 Delian triplet turns
73 *The Road to Samarkand*, (Jahoda) p. 198.

54 Delian Soaring-triplet - sol-la-do mi
74 *Frederick Delius*, (Beecham) p. 73.
75 *The Road to Samarkand*, (Jahoda) p. 60.
76 *In slavery, some holler..... Slave Narrative Collection*, (Southern) p.117.
77 ibid
78 *Frederick Delius*, (Warlock & Foss) p. 143.

57 Group I: Possum up a Gum Tree and other songs
79 *Dan Emmett and the Rise of Early Negro Minstrelsy*, (Nathan) pp. 44-48.
80 Dorothy Scarborough, *On the trail of Negro Folk Songs* (Cambridge, Mass: Harvard University Press, 1923), p. 162.

58 Group II: Anacrusis/snap tunes
81 Thomas Edward Bowdich, 'Mission from Cape Coast Castle to Ashantee,' (London,1819), repr. in Southern *Readings*, p.8.
82 E. A. McIlhenny, *Befo' de War Spirituals* (Boston: The Christopher Publishing House, 1933), p. 12.

68 Group IX: 'Marching through Georgia' themes
83 *Slave Songs of the United States*, (Allen, Ware & Garrison) p. 45 (foot-note).
84 *On the trail of Negro Folk Songs*, (Scarborough) p. 162.

69 Introduction to Part Five
85 'Memories of Delius,' (Redwood) p. 140.
86 *This and other ...... Delius as I knew him*, (Fenby) p. 25.

74 Koanga [1895/7]
87 *Frederick Delius*, (Beecham) p. 82.

76 Piano Concerto [1897, re. 1904, 1906-7 and 1909]
88 *When he was about twenty .....* W. H. Humiston, The Philharmonic Society of New York, concert programme for November 26th., 1915.
89 New York: *The Sun*, Nov. 27th, 1915, also New York: *The New York Times*, Nov. 22nd, 1915, also New York: *Town and Country*, Dec. 10th, 1915.

77 Appalachia [1898-1903]
90 'Delius in America,' (Redwood) p. 160.
91 Harry T. Burleigh (ed), *Negro Minstrel Melodies* (New York: G. Schirmer, c. 1909) and *The Spirituals of Harry T. Burleigh*, (Miami: Belwin Mills, 1984).
92 *American Negro Spirituals*. (Johnson & Johnson)
93 Dena J. Epstein, *Sinful Tunes and Spirituals* (Urbana: University of Illinois Press, 1977). pp. 260-270, and Appendix III.

80 Mass of Life [1904-5]
94 *In thine eye .....* Friedrich Nietzsche, *Also Sprach Zarathustra*, (trans. John Bernhoff) text of Frederick Delius, *A Mass of Life*, (opening of movement III) (Berlin: Harmonie Verlag, 1906/7, repr. London: Boosey and Hawkes, 1952).

83 In a Summer Garden [1907]
95 *Roses, lilies, ...* preface to Universal Edition score, 1921. Quoted in English in Gloria Jahoda *The Road to Samarkand*, (New York: Charles Scrivener's Sons, 1969), p. 158.

86   The Song of the High Hills [1911]
96   *On the trail of Negro Folk Songs,* (Scarborough) pp. 125-127.
97   *Slave Songs of the United States,* (Allen, Ware & Garrison) p. 45 (footnote).

92   Air and Dance [1913]
98   *Philip had rekindled ..... The Road to Samarkand,* (Jahoda) p. 180.

93   Double Concerto [1915-16]
99   *The Road to Samarkand,* (Jahoda) p, 181.

95   Violin Concerto [1916]
100   *Delius as I knew him,* (Fenby) p. 195.

98   String Quartet [1916-17]
101   'The Personality of Frederick Delius,' (Redwood) pp. 120-121.

104   A Song of Summer [1929]
102   *I want you to imagine..... Delius as I knew him,* (Fenby) p. 132.

109   In the Evening by the Moonlight
103   *The Music of Black Americans,* (Southern) pp. 234-237.

Bibliography

together with notes on the collections most often used in this study.

African and Afro-American Music

Allen, William Francis, Charles Pickard Ware and Lucy McKim Garrison. *Slave Songs of the United States.* New York: A. Simpson & Co., 1867. Repr. New York: Arno Press, 1971.
　　Melody and text only. The first extensive study of Afro-American song, collected immediately after the Civil War. Divided into different sections devoted to songs of the Southeastern Slave States, Northern Slave States, Inland Slave States and the Gulf States. Contains a very important Introduction.

AME Church. *The Hymnbook of the African Methodist Episcopalian Church.* Philadelphia: Publication Department of the AME Church, 1873.

Barton, William Eleazer. 'Old Plantation Hymns,' *New England Magazine,* December, 1898. Repr. in Katz.

_____ 'Hymns of the Slave and Freedman,' *New England Magazine,* January, 1899. Repr. in Katz.

_____ 'Recent Negro Melodies,' *New England Magazine,* February, 1899. Repr. in Katz.

Borroff, Edith. *Music in Europe and the United States: A Panorama.* Englewood Cliffs, NJ: Prentice-Hall Inc., 1971.

Brown, John Mason. 'Songs of the Slave,' *Lippincott's Magazine,* December, 1868. Repr. in Katz.

Burleigh, Harry T., ed. *Negro Minstrel Melodies.* New York: G. Schirmer, 1910.

Burlin, Natalie Curtis. *Hampton series Negro folk-songs.* New York: G. Schirmer, c.1918/19.
　　Important and detailed notations of mainly secular songs from the singing of a male vocal quartet.

_____ 'Black Singers and Players,' *The Musical Quarterly,* October, 1919.

Cable, George Washington. 'Creole Slave Songs,' *The Century Magazine,* April, 1886. Repr. in Katz.

_____ 'The Dance in Place Congo,' *The Century Magazine,* February, 1886. Repr. in Katz.

Carawan, Guy (ed.). *Been in the Storm so Long.* [LP] New York: Folkways Records, (LP FS 3842) 1967.

Christensen, Abigail M. Holmes. 'Spirituals and 'Shouts' of Southern Negroes,' Philadelphia: *Journal of American Folk-Lore - 7,* 1894.

Church Hymnal Corporation, the. *Lift Every Voice and Sing - An African American Hymnal.* [LEVAS] New York: The Episcopal Church, 1981.

Church Music Corporation, the. *Lift Every Voice and Sing II - An African American Hymnal.* [LEVAS] New York: The Episcopal Church, 1993.

Courlander, Harold. *A Treasury of Afro-American Folklore.* New York: Crown Publishers, 1976.

_____ *Negro Songs from Alabama.* 2nd ed. New York: Oak Publications, 1963.

_____ *Negro Folk Music.* New York: Columbia University Press, 1963.

Dett, R. Nathaniel. *Religious Folk Songs of the Negro as sung at the Hampton Institute.* Hampton, VA: The Institute Press, 1927.

Epstein, Dena J. *Sinful Tunes and Spirituals.* Chicago: University of Illinois Press, 1971.

_____ *White Origin for the Black Spirituals.* Champaign, IL: American Music - Summer 1983.

Fenner, Thomas P. *Religious Folk Songs of the Negro.* Hampton, VA: The Institute Press, 1920.
    Melodies and harmonizations collected from the singing of the students of the Hampton Institute, Hampton, Virginia. No secular songs and very little chromaticism or modulation in the harmony voices.

Floyd, Samuel, and Marsha Reisser. *Black Music in the United States - An Annotated Bibliography.* Millwood, NY: Kraus International Publishing, 1983.

Garrison, Lucy McKim. 'Songs of the Port Royal 'Contrabands',' Boston: *Dwight's Journal of Music,* 8th November, 1862. Repr. in Katz.

Gershwin, George, and Ira Gershwin. *Porgy and Bess - An American Folk Opera.* New York: Gershwin Publishing Corp., 1935.

Hallowell, Emily. *Calhoun Plantation Songs.* 2nd edition Boston: C. W. Thompson & Co., 1907.
    Collected from the singing of students at the Calhoun Colored School in the Black belt of Alabama. A mixture of secular and religious songs notated mainly in four voices but with many in two or three parts. No voices added by the editor. Important from the light it sheds on Afro-American part singing style and practices.

Haskell, Marion Alexander. 'Negro 'Spirituals',' *The Century Magazine* XXXVI, August, 1899. Repr. in Katz.

Higginson, Thomas Wentworth. 'Negro Spirituals,' *The Atlantic Monthly* XIX, June, 1867. Repr. in Katz.

Howard, John Tasker. 'Capturing the Spirit of the Real Negro Music; First Accurate Recordings by Natalie Curtis-Burlin of Negro part singing,' New York: *The Musician,* 24, 1919.

Humiston, W. H. Program Notes for the Concert on November 26th, 1915. New York: New York Philharmonic Orchestra, 1915.

Hungerford, James. *The Old Plantation.* New York: Harper, 1859.

Hundley, Daniel. *Social Relations in Our Southern States.* New York: H. B. Price, 1860.

Jackson, Bruce. *Wake Up Dead Man.* Cambridge, MA: Harvard University Press, 1972.
    Very fully transcribed with detailed ornamentation. A number of the songs are in two or three voices. No added voices. It is doubtful if this style of singing has changed much over the past hundred years although many of the melodies and texts would be recent additions to the general canon.

Jackson, Irene V. *Afro-American Religious Music - A Bibliography and A Catalogue of Gospel Music.* Westport, CT: Greenwood Press Inc., 1979.

Jackson, Marylou India, *Negro Spirituals and Hymns*. New York: J. Fischer, c.1935.

James, Willis Laurence. 'The Romance of the Negro Folk Cry in America,' Atlanta: *Phylon* - University of Atlanta, Ist. Qt., 1955.

Jessup, Lynn Elva. *African Characteristics found in Afro-American and Anglo-American Music*. (M.A. Thesis), Seattle, WA: University of Washington, 1971.

Johnson, James Weldon and J. Rosamond Johnson. *American Negro Spirituals*. 1925 2nd Ed. New York: Da Capo Press Inc., 1981.
> The standard solo voice and piano collection. Primarily arranged for parlour or concert use: all of the songs traditional and well-known. Contains an important introduction.

Jones, A. M. *Studies in African Music*. London: Oxford University Press, 1959.

Johns, Altona Trent. *Play Songs of the Deep South*. Washington: The Associated Publishers, 1944.

Katz, Bernard, ed. *The Social Implications of Early Negro Music in the United States: with over 150 of the Songs, Many of Them with Their Music*. New York: Arno Press, 1969.
> An anthology of articles published in the years immediately following the Civil War. Text and melody line only. Included are:
> I   'Negro Songs' (1862) - James Miller Mc Kim
> II   'Negro 'Shouts' and Shout Songs' (1863) - H. G. Spaulding
> III 'Songs of the Port Royal 'Contrabands'' (1862) - Lucy McKim Garrison
> IV 'Negro Spirituals' (1867) - Thomas Wentworth Higginson
> V   'Songs of the Slave' (1868) - James Mason Brown
> VI 'The Dance in Place Congo' (1886) and *Creole Slave Songs* (1886) - George Washington Cable
> VII 'Negro Camp-Meeting Melodies' (1892) - Henry Cleveland Wood
> VIII 'Old Plantation Hymns,' (1898), 'Hymns of the Slave and the Freedman' (1899) and 'Recent Negro-Melodies' (1899) - William Eleazer Barton.
> IX 'Negro Spirituals' (1899) - Marion Alexander Haskell
> X   'The Social Implications of the Negro Spiritual' (1939) - John Lovell, Jr.

Kennedy, R. Emmet. *Mellows: A Chronicle of Unknown Singers*. New York: Albert & Charles Boni, c.1925.

_____ *More Mellows*. New York: Dodd, Mead and Company, 1931.

Kingman, Daniel. *American Music*. New York: G. Schirmer Inc., 1979.

Kirby, Percival R. *A Study of Negro Harmony*. New York: The Musical Quarterly, 16, 1930.

Krehbiel, Henry Edward. *Afro-American Folksongs: A Study in Racial and National Music*. New York: G. Schirmer, Inc., 1914.
> Probably the earliest attempt at a rational analysis of Afro-American vocal/choral music since the work of Allen, Ware and Garrison in 1867, together with examples of songs and spirituals,

Leiding, Harriette Kershaw. *Street Cries of an Old Southern City*. Charleston, SC: The Daggett Printing Co., 1910.

Lomax, John A. and Alan Lomax. *American Ballads and Folk Songs*. New York: The Macmillan Company, 1934.

_____ *Negro Folk Songs as sung by Lead Belly.* New York: The Macmillan Company, 1936.

Lowell, John Jnr. 'The Social Implications of the Negro Spiritual,' *Journal of Negro Education,* October, 1939. Repr. in Katz.

Marsh, J. B. T. and F. J. Loudin. *The Story of The Jubilee Singers, with Supplement.* London: Hodder and Stoughton, 1902.
  Almost all the examples are religious; being either spirituals or jubilee hymns. Mostly arranged for four parts, although some consist only of the melody. The chording is very simple, almost totally diatonic and very effective.

Maultsby, Portia Katrenia. *Afro-American Religious Music - 1619-1861.[Part I Historical Development, Part II Computer Analysis.]* (Ph.D Thesis, University of Wisconsin, 1974.) Westport, CT: Greenwood Press, c.1979.

McIlhenny, E. A. *Befo' de War Spirituals.* Boston: The Christopher Publishing House, 1933.
  Collected from singing of two very elderly plantation workers on an estate at Avery Island, in an isolated area in the sugar-belt of Louisiana. A large collection mainly arranged for solo or unison singing and piano. Many different songs, mostly with a 'revivalist' feel to them. A colorful and informative introduction.

McKim, James Miller. 'Negro Songs,' Boston: *Dwight's Journal of Music,* 9th August, 1862. Repr. in Katz.

Miller, Terry. *Folk Music in America (A Reference Guide).* New York: Garland Publishing, 1986.

National Baptist Convention of America. *National Jubilee Melodies.* Nashville, TN: National Baptist Pub. Board, 19??.

Nettl, Bruno. *Folk and Traditional Music of the Western Continents.* Englewood Cliffs, NJ: Prentice-Hall, Inc., 1965.

Nketia, J.H. Kwabena. *The Music of Africa.* New York: W. W. Norton & Company, 1974.
  An important text, indispensable for those interested in the music of West Africa.

Odum, Howard Washington, and Garry B. Johnson. *Negro Workaday Songs.* Chapel Hill, NC: University of North Carolina Press, 1926.

Parrish, Lydia. *Slave Songs of the Georgia Sea Islands.* New York: Creative Age Press, 1942.
  Collected by Lydia A. Parrish and transcribed by Creighton Churchill and Robert MacGimsey. Again a collection from an isolated location giving a different slant to the genre. Mainly secular songs consisting of either solo voice or for solo voice with accompanying singers (basers). The style travels the distance from African melody through English 18th century catch songs to Spirituals and Jubilee style hymns.

Parth, Johnny. *The Earliest Negro Vocal Quartets: Volume 1 (1894-1928).* [CD] Vienna, Austria: Document Records (DOCD-5061), 1991.

_____ *The Earliest Negro Vocal Groups: Volume 2 (1895-1922).* [CD] Vienna, Austria: Document Records (DOCD-5288), 1994.

Peabody, Charles. 'Notes on Negro Music,' Philadelphia: *Journal of American Folklore* 16, July, 1903.

Ricks, George Robinson. *Some Aspects of the Religious Music of the U.S. Negro.* c.1960, (Thesis, Northwestern University) New York: Arno Press, 1977.

Rodeheaver, Homer. *Rodeheaver's Negro Spirituals*. Philadelphia: Rodeheaver, c.1923.

Scarborough, Dorothy. *On the Trail of Negro Folk-Songs*. Cambridge, MA: Harvard University Press, 1925.
    The first important collection devoted mainly to the field of secular song - in the main, text and melody only.

Silverman, Jerry. *Slave Songs*. New York: Chelsea House Publishers, 1994.

Southern, Eileen. *The Music of Black Americans*. New York: W. W. Norton & Company, 1971.
    The standard late twentieth century text.

_____ ed. *Readings in Black American Music*. New York: W. W. Norton & Company, 1971.
    A useful companion to Katz, complete with the earliest notations of African music. Contains virtually all important historical writings spanning the seventeenth to the twentieth centuries, such as excerpts from Mungo Park's *Travels in the Interior Districts of Africa*, Thomas Edward Bowdich's *Mission from Cape Coast Castle to Ashantee*, James Hungerford's *The Old Plantation*, and Thomas W. Higginson's *Army Life in a Black Regiment*.

Spaeth, Sigmund. *Barber Shop Ballads and how to sing them*. New York: Simon and Schuster, 1925, repr. Prentice-Hall, Inc. 1940.

Spaulding, Henry George. 'Negro 'Shouts' and Shout Songs,' *Continental Monthly*, August, 1863. Repr. in Katz.

Taylor, Marshall W. and Josephine Robinson. *A Collection of Revival Hymns and plantation melodies*. Cincinnati: Marshall W. Taylor and W. C. Echols, Publishers, 1883.
    Collected by Marshall W. Taylor with accompaniments by Amelia C. and Hettie G. Taylor. Black and white hymns sung at the Rev. Taylor's church in Cincinnati. An 'amateur' collection with notational mistakes, but nevertheless of historical interest.

Titon, Jeff Todd. *Early Downhome Blues*. Chicago: University of Chicago Press, 1977.

Waterman, Richard A. 'African Influence on the music of the Americas, Acculturation in the Americas,' *Proceedings of the 29th International Congress of Americanists*, Sol Tax, ed. Chicago: University of Chicago Press, 1952.
_____ 'On Flogging a Dead Horse: Lessons learned from the Africanisms Controversy,' Champaign, IL: *Ethnomusicology* 7, 1963.

Wheeler, Mary. *Steamboatin' Days: Folk Songs of the River Packet Era*. Baton Rouge, LA: Louisiana State University Press, 1944.
    Collected from the singing of several very elderly riverboat workers. Melody and text only, the majority of the songs are secular and most of them are in an early idiom. Probably the most useful text for my study.

Wheeler, Mary, and William J. Reddick. *Roustabout Songs*. New York: Remick Music Corp., c.1939.

Williams, Thelma A. *Origin and Analysis of Negro Folk-Song*. Detroit, MI: M.S, Thesis, Wayne State University, 1938.

Wood, Henry Cleveland. 'Negro Camp-Meeting Melodies,' *New England Magazine*. March, 1892. Repr. in Katz.

Work, John Wesley. *Folk Song of The American Negro*. 1915. New York: Negro Universities Press, 1969.

Work, John W. *American Negro Songs.* New York: Crown Publishers Inc., 1940.
> A late collection, mainly spirituals, but also with ballads and work songs. The spirituals are harmonized in four parts with almost totally diatonic harmony. The secular songs consist of the melody-line only. Contains an important Introduction. Although published some seventy-five years after FD's sojourn in the US, the majority of these songs would have been in existence in the 1880s.

White-American and European Music

Abbott, Lynn. ' 'Play That Barber Shop Chord': A Case for the African-American Origin of Barbershop Harmony,' *American Music* Fall 1992. Champaign, IL: University of Illinois.

Biancolli, Louis and William S. Mann. *The Analytical Concert Guide.* London: Cassell & Company Ltd., 1957. Repr. Westport, CN: Greenwood Press, 1971.

Bridge, Sir Frederick. *The Old Cryes of London.* London: Novello and Company, Limited, 1921.

Browne, Ray B. 'Some Notes on the Southern 'Holler',' Philadelphia: *Journal of American Folklore* 67, 1954.

Buchan, Norman and Peter Hall. *The Scottish Folksinger.* London: Collins, 1973.

'Chaff, Gumbo' (Elias Howe). *The Ethiopian Glee Book.* Boston: Elias Howe, 1848.

Creighton, Helen and Calum MacLeod. *Gaelic Songs in Nova Scotia.* Ottawa: National Museum of Canada, 1979.

Damon, S. Foster. *Old American Songs.* Providence, R. I: Brown University Library, 1936.

Davis, Joe. *Georgia Minstrel and Entertainment Folio.* New York: Georgia Music Corp., 1940.

Foster, Stephen, *77 Stephen Foster Songs.* 1939. Chicago: M. M. Cole Publishing Co., 1966.

Hicks, Val. 'Barbershop Quartet Singing,' *The New Grove Dictionary of American Music.* New York: Grove Dictionary of Music, 1986.

Hudson, Winthrop S. 'Shouting Methodists,' *Encounter* 29, 1968.

Lawrence, Vera Brodsky. *Music for Patriots, Politicians, and Presidents.* New York: MacMillan Publishing Co., Inc., 1975.

Martin, C. T. 'Deac'. 'The Evolution of Barbershop Harmony,' *Music Journal Annual Anthology* 23, 1965.

Nathan, Hans. *Dan Emmett and the Rise of Early Negro Minstrelsy.* Norman, OK: University of Oklahoma Press, c.1962.

Neale, R. H. and H. W. Day. *Revival Hymns.* Boston: Hartley Wood, Publisher, 1842.

Spaeth, Sigmund. *Barber Shop Ballads.* New York: Prentice-Hall, Inc., 1940.

Szabo, Burt. *Heritage of Harmony Songbook.* Kenosha, WI: Society for the Preservation and
        Encouragement of Barber Shop Quartet Singing in America, Inc., 1988.

White, C.A. and Sam Lucas. *Plantation songs and jubilee hymns.* Chicago & Boston: White, Smith & Co.,
        1881.

The Delius Circle

Beecham, Sir Thomas. *A Mingled Chime.* London: Hutchinson and Co. Ltd., 1944.

_____ *Frederick Delius.* New York: Alfred A. Knopf, 1960.

Bird, John. *Percy Grainger.* London; Elek Books Ltd., 1976.

Carley, Lionel and Robert Threlfall. *Delius: A Life in Pictures.* Oxford: Oxford University Press, 1977.

Carley, Lionel. *Delius: A Life in Letters (volume I).* London: Scholar Press, 1983.

Delius, Clare. *Frederick Delius: Memories of My Brother.* London: I. Nicholson & Watson, 1935.

Fenby, Eric. *Delius as I knew him.* 1936. London: Quality Press Ltd., 1948.

Foreman, Lewis. *The Percy Grainger Companion.* London: Thames, 1981.

Gray, Cecil. 'Memories of Delius,' *Musical Chairs.* London: Home and van Thal, 1948.

Hutchings, Arthur. *Delius.* 1948. London: MacMillan & Co. Ltd., 1949.

Jahoda, Gloria. *The Other Florida.* New York: Charles Scribner's Sons, 1967.

_____ *The Road to Samarkand.* New York: Charles Scribner's Sons, 1969.

Lowe, Rachel. *Delius Collection of the Grainger Museum.* London: The Delius Trust, 1980.

Palmer, Christopher. *Delius Portrait of a Cosmopolitan.* London: Duckworth, 1976.

Redwood, Christopher, ed. *A Delius Companion.* 1976. London: John Calder, 1980.

Threllfall, Robert. *A Catalogue of the Compositions of Frederick Delius.* London: Delius Trust, 1977.

_____ 'Delius:- Late Swallows in Florida,' London: *The Composer* 51, Spring 1974

Warlock, Peter (Philip Heseltine) with additions by Hubert Foss,. *Frederick Delius.* London: The Bodley Head,
1923 rev. 1952.

Index of Musical Examples

(Numbers refer to the music examples, those in *italics* refer to composite examples).

70   *Florida*   [1887/89]
I   Daybreak   1 m. before cue 2 (hns)   148
I   Daybreak   7 ms. before cue 3 (ob)   13
I   Daybreak   7 ms. after cue 3 (vls I & II)   45
I   Daybreak   4 ms. before cue 8 (flts)   75
III   Sunset (Danza) cue 3 (strgs)   8, *117*
III   Sunset (Danza) 1 m. after cue 3 (vls I & II)   *139*
III   Sunset cue 4 (ob)   177
IV   At Night m. 15 (hn)   61

71   *Twilight Fancies* [1890]
cadence at m. 14 (pf & voice)   3

72   *Summer Evening* [1890]
opening (fl)   *109b*

73   *Irmelin* [1890-2] (Vocal score)
I   opening (*Pf*, r.h., upper voice)   52, *76*
I   m. 20 (*Pf*, r.h., upper voice)   *76, 158,*
I   Prelude-closing (*Pf*, r.h., upper voice)   172, 202
I   m. 135 (A Maid) *Never was there maid like thee....*   182, *166*
I   m. 331 (*Pf*, r.h., upper voice)   154
II   m. 231 (*Pf*, l.h., upper voice)   23, *155*
II   m. 613 (*Pf*, r.h., lower voice & l.h. upper voice)   *153*
II   m. 756 (*Pf*, both staves)   63
III   m. 39 (*Pf*, r.h., upper voice)   183
III   m. 42 (*Pf*, r.h., upper voice)   135, *139*
III   m. 391 (Irmelin) *How beautiful and silent*   62
III   m. 393 (*Pf*, r.h., upper voice)   *132f*
IV   m. 1044 (Nils) *Fare thee well, Oh! sweet silver stream*   173

74   *Koanga* [1895/7]
Prologue 11 ms. after cue 2 ('cellos)   *178*
I   8 ms. before cue 6 (fl & cl)   46
I   9 ms. after cue 17 ('cello)   118
I   cue 26 - *Pa, he said* (chorus-sop)   20
I   cue 28 - *I feel a strange foreboding* (Palmyra)   67
I   6 ms. before cue 29 (ww)   47
II   opening - *Now once in a while* (chorus-sop)   66, *180*
II   cue 2 (ww)   181, *202*
II   12 ms. before cue 3 *He will meet her* (chorus-sop)   *166*
III   4 m. before cue 10 - *Voodoo hear!* (Rangwan)   *84*
III   7 ms. after cue 13 (vl)   115
III   closing (ob & hn)   *84*, 94, *202*

75   *Romance* for cello and piano [1896]
m. 3 (cello)   123
m. 67 (cello)   184

76 Piano Concerto [1897/1904-9]
   Opening subject (vln I)   38, *76, 126, 153*
   cue 3 (pf)   71
   Second subject 3 m. after 3 (hn/pf/vln)   82, *117*
   Second subject (hn)   *140*
   Largo - cue 14 (pf)   58, *90*

77 Appalachia   [1898-1903]
   Variation Theme (c. angl & bns)   6, *119a, 166*
   4 ms. before cue C (hp & vla/bn)   9
   2 m. before cue B (cl)   122
   cue J (cello)   141

78 A Village Romeo and Juliet [1900/01]
I opening (vl II)   14
I opening (cl/vl I)   57
I 3 ms. after cue 1 (c.angl/bn/hns/vla)   156
I 3 ms. after cue 5 (ob)   151
II cue 17 (Vrenchen) - *I go t'wards evening*   *119a*, 186
IV cue 6 (Vrenchen) - *Ah the night*   *119b*, 187
VI opening (Chorus-sop) - *Dance along*   53
VI cue 84 (Vagabond I) - *Vagabonds are we!*   88

78a The Walk to the Paradise Garden
   opening (bsn/hn)   18
   5 ms. after cue I (ob)   64
   1 m. after cue 2 (cl)   120
   cue 15 (flts)   145

79 Sea Drift [1903/4]
   cue 3 (ob)   103
   3 ms. before cue 22 (hn)   128, *132a*

80 Mass of Life [1904/5]
III m. 2 (chorus--altos)   97
III cue 19 (chorus-altos)   15, *139*

81 Songs of Sunset [1906/7]
   6 ms. after cue 4 (ft/c. angl)   188, *132f*
   cue 15 (fl/ob)   187
   cue 30 (cor angl.)   39
   4 ms. before cue 41 (chorus)   73
   closing (chorus/strings)   190

82 Brigg Fair [1907]
   opening (fl/cl)   100, *132d*
   1 m. after cue 9 (vl I)   10

83 In a Summer Garden [1908 rev. 1911]
   m. 6 (ob)   136, *139*
   6 ms. after cue 11 (fl & ob)   191

96	*Violin Concerto* [1916]	
	opening (vl I)	147
	m.3 (solo vl)	48, *132e*
	cue 12 (solo vl)	202
	5 m. after 14 (solo vl)	129, *132a*
	cue 15 (solo vl & strgs)	65
	cue 19 (vl I)	35, *126*
	cue 32 (solo vl)	11
97	*Cello Sonata* [1916]	
	opening (pf)	204
	m. 25 (cello)	176
	m. 45 (pf)	*205*
	m. 127 (cello)	*155, 205*
	m. 141 (cello)	*205*
98	*String Quartet* [1916/17]	
I	close (vl I)	49, *206*
II	opening (vl I)	*206,*
III	not too slow and with waving movement (vl I)	12
III	6 ms. after cue 4 (vl I)	179
III	2 ms. before cue 8 (vl I)	72
III	2 ms. after cue 5 (vl I)	*119b*
IV	m.10 (vl I)	77
IV	4 ms. before cue 3 (cello)	83, *139*
IV	3 ms. before 21 (vl I)	*84*, 92
99	*To be sung of a summer night on the water* [1917]	
II	opening (tenor solo)	54, *132a, 139*
100	*A Song before Sunrise* [1918]	-
101	*Intermezzo* and *Serenade* from *Hassan* [1920/23]	
	Intermezzo - opening (solo cello)	131, *132c*
	m. 5 (cl)	*208*
	Serenade - opening (vl I)	*84, 93*
102	*Cello Concerto* [1921]	
	m. 36 (solo cello)	85, *202*
	m. 90 (vl I)	81
	m. 158 (vl I & cellos)	89
	m. 185 (solo cello)	174, *202*
	m. 277 (fl/vl I & II)	175
	m. 290 (solo cello)	22, *132c, 208*
103	*Violin Sonata II* [1923]	
	Poco meno mosso (pf)	169
	2 ms. after poco meno mosso (vl)	209
	Piu tranquillo e piu lento (vl)	106

The Delius Society

The Delius Society, Philadelphia Branch, Inc., was founded December 11. 1976 as a branch of the British Delius Society. Incorporated in 1978 as a non-profit 501 (c) (3) educational organization, it has been independent since that year. The Delius Society seeks a wider appreciation of the music of Frederick Delius and his contemporaries. Each year The Delius Society presents a variety of public concerts, film programs, lectures, symposia and often cooperates and encourages other performers or ensembles to perform Delius works. Social activities often accompany these events. *The Delian* is published three times a year.

The Delius Society maintains a large library of scores, books, videos/films, and recordings, which serves as the primary resource for British music in Philadelphia. Upon appointment, researchers or those preparing public performances may examine The Delius Society holdings.

Annual memberships are $15 with Life memberships also available at $250. For further information contact

The Delius Society,
c/o Arthur D. Zbinden,
1540, Grovania Avenue,
Abington, PA 19001

The Author

Derek Healey was born in Wargrave, England in 1936, and studied composition with Herbert Howells at the Royal College of Music, London and with Boris Porena and Gofredo Petrassi in Italy. He has won prizes in the UK, Italy and the USA and has taught Theory, Composition and Ethnic Music at the Universities of Victoria, Toronto, Guelph and Oregon, finally becoming Academic Professor of Music at the RAF School of Music in Uxbridge, England. He has written works in most genres, having had some forty-five works published in the UK, Canada and the USA. Works for large ensembles have been played by fifteen orchestras or wind ensembles, and the opera *Seabird Island* was the first contemporary opera to be taken on a cross-Canada tour. Healey, who is a Fellow of the Royal College of Organists and has his doctorate from the University of Toronto, is now retired from teaching and spends his time with composition and research, residing in the Cobble Hill district of Brooklyn, New York.